HERMANN BECKH (1875–1 Sanskrit, becoming Professor University of Berlin. A mast languages, he wrote extensively on religious and philosophical subjects, including Buddhism, Indology, Christianity, Alchemy and Music. In 1911, he heard a lecture by Rudolf Steiner and was inspired to join the Anthroposophical Society, where he soon became a valued co-worker. In 1922, he helped found The Christian Community, a movement for religious renewal. His many books are gradually being translated from the original German and published in English.

ALCHYMY

The Mystery of the Material World

Hermann Beckh

Translated from the German by Maren & Alan Stott
Edited with a Introduction by Neil Franklin

TEMPLE LODGE

Temple Lodge Publishing Ltd.
Hillside House, The Square
Forest Row, RH18 5ES

www.templelodge.com

Published in English by Temple Lodge 2019

Originally published in German under the title *Alchymie, Vom Geheimnis der Stoffeswelt*, Geering Verlag, Dornach 1931

This edition © Temple Lodge Publishing 2019
Translation © Alan & Maren Stott 2019

A CIP catalogue record for this book is available from the British Library

ISBN 978 1 912230 35 8

Cover by Morgan Creative
Typeset by DP Photosetting, Neath, West Glamorgan
Printed and bound by 4Edge Ltd., Essex

Contents

Foreword

This short work only intends to be regarded as an introduction to a distant future search. It is addressed to those who in the midst of the present darkness have retained something of the primeval longing of mankind, of an intuition for the Mysteries, and who are still able to sense the reality in fairy-tales. It especially addresses knowledgeable readers of the book issued by the same publisher, *John's Gospel: The Cosmic Rhythm – Stars and Stones* (Leominster: Anastasi 2015; hereafter JG) to which it forms a kind of Appendix, a supplementary chapter, and also touches some of the issues that in the short work *Our Origin in the Light* (Leominster: Anastasi 2015; Temple Lodge, forthcoming) as well as the poetic piece *The New Jerusalem* (see Appendix). The present work addresses those who condense into thought what is physically not yet graspable, fashioning this into meditative thinking, and who want to make this meditative, spiritual content their own. Last but not least, it is also for those who seek a spiritual-physical, scientific explanation, for the Mystery of metamorphosis (transubstantiation) and for sacramental life in general.

Where the results of independent spiritual research by Rudolf Steiner are included, the presentation here clearly recognizes this, as well as all other sources. Such inclusions are never meant dogmatically, but always with the attitude that everything referred to can be understood by thinking it out for oneself. It can also be seen how with such references the additions are decisive for the leading themes, the meditative construction of the thoughts and the content of the whole exposition.

For certain indications with the colour-grouping of the 'twelve gem-stones', the author thanks Frl. Völker (Stuttgart) and for indications to certain lesser-known and less accessible alchemical writings thanks to the Baroness v. Bernus (Stuttgart). For an indication of a passage on the Mystery of wine and the wedding at Cana in *Die Geheimen Figuren der Rosenkreutzer* ['Secret Figures of the Rosicrucians'], my thanks to Herrn Wilhelm Petersen (Darmstadt). Finally, for pointing out a lecture by Dr Rudolf Steiner mentioned in the Appendix, my thanks extend to Dr Friedrich Rittelmeyer (Stuttgart).

Warm gratitude to my publisher Herr Rudolf Geering, who was able to publish this work so soon after the appearance of the above-mentioned larger book and in difficult times.

Hermann Beckh
Stuttgart, 13 February 1931

Introduction

Hermann Beckh's small book on the mystery of substance, or 'Alchymie' as he chose to represent the traditions of philosophical alchemy, has proved to be one of his most popular publications, running through five editions in 1931, 1937, 1942, 2007 and 2013. At first written as a helpful 'appendix' to the major volumes on the Gospels of Mark (1928) and John (1930), particularly to illuminate the resurrection and then the New Jerusalem in Revelation, it became a substantial work standing by itself, dealing with the most essential themes.

The first edition was published by Hermann Geering in Basel inside a handsome leaf-green cover with gold letters and alchemical symbols. Whether it was that Beckh's major gospel studies were either too large or too complex, The Christian Community Press in the basement of the priests' seminar house, directed by Friedrich Rittelmeyer, had declined the publishing of these immense investigations. The publisher, however, recognized Beckh's commanding genius: perhaps they used to meet at Geering's home 'im Wiesengrund' at Binnengen, just outside Basel where Rudolf Steiner's masonic rituals continued working during the 1920s.[1]

When one surveys the in-house publications of the young Christian Community between 1922 and 1931 and Beckh's legacy today the first unavoidable impression is that the primary authors, Rittelmeyer, Bock and a little later Rudolf Frieling, successfully built up the 'Reformation reformed' centred in Stuttgart by extended commentaries on both the Old and New Testaments. With his huge experience in the Lutheran-Evangelical Church, Friedrich Rittelmeyer was adept at calling to the human heart to embrace the new life in Christ; Emil Bock devoted his abundant youthful energies to re-translating the New Testament and applying Imaginative insights to the whole of Scripture. While these approaches did indeed build up the nascent community in a worthy fashion, consolidating its foundations, they were largely limited to Lutheran perspectives and the history of the Western Church. It is quite different with Beckh: here Christianity, the Mystery of Golgotha, is renewed from professorial knowledge of Sanskrit, Pali and Avestan coupled with a musical soul plus a meditative penetration of star-signs and planets. Beckh's range with his knowledge of ancient languages was largely beyond the comprehension of his colleagues, who were often dumbfounded.[2]

Nevertheless this is not the main point, as something still more resonant comes to light after living with Beckh for many years. As Rittelmeyer, Bock and Frieling co-founded The Christian Community in the 1920s one can observe that they were fully on course in applying their knowledge and skills to the contemporary situation. But this was not enough for Beckh. By a strange polarity, the investigation of the most ancient texts from India and Iran out of meditative soundings came above all to constitute a compelling invitation to *future work*— something that seriously challenges us today, a hundred years later. To be quite clear, Beckh's studies, whether books or articles, consistently look to a future that yearns to make its presence a reality.

Yet for the young Christian Community, still only in its ninth year in 1931, it was imperative to consolidate a renewed understanding of the sacraments, starting in the Stuttgart Seminary where Beckh was teaching. From the broadly German side, one could say, there was indeed the Grail tradition, but from the specifically Lutheran side (the religious background of the majority of founding priests)[3] there was some interest in Jakob Böhme (1575–1624), the one Christian visionary philosopher within the Reformed churches who stands closest to anthroposophy, apart from the fact that the influence of Böhme was immense on Novalis, Louis Claude de Saint-Martin, Oetinger and Fabre d'Olivet, who were all of interest to Hermann Beckh.

The early apologists for The Christian Community, centred in the Stuttgart Seminary, understood that they were heirs of a Germanic Rosicrucian tradition as expressed in Rudolf Steiner's lectures on the subject, but the vast debt that this tradition owed to Böhme was largely overlooked. In fact, the dependence of the above writers, not to mention Fichte and Hegel, was totally overriding. It is as though the younger generation in the 1920s and 30s looked primarily to Steiner without recognizing the potential of their older inheritance.

From a historical point of view, there are Rudolf Steiner's indications that Böhme was closely linked to the Rosicrucian movement, and was thereby initiated into his life-task shortly before 1612.[4] Exoterically, it is a matter of simple empirical observation to notice that Böhme did belong to some kind of secret society, evidenced by the use of code in the *Aurora* of 1612, and that his writings when edited and published by Gichtel formed the backbone of both European and New World Rosicrucian societies culminating in the foundation of the Euphrata Community in Pennsylvania through Johannes Kelpius.[5] There is not a shadow of doubt that the vast majority of eighteenth century Rosicrucian texts, including those mentioned here in *Alchymie*, are heavily dependent on Böhme as mediated, for example, by Gichtel, Freher and J.J. Zimmermann. Both Böhme's writings and the derivative publications within this tradition then came to the notice of Goethe and also the Idealist philosophers between 1790 and 1815.

What this all suggests is that for three centuries, with or without Rosicrucian spiritual practice, most of Europe and Russia found that this new kind of Christianity to make itself understood required its own distinctive vocabulary and philosophy whose original source was Böhme. Here it would be only glib to say that Böhme had some kind of 'lasting appeal'; there was something more profound at work. For certain pioneering spirits, whether the earlier George Fox and William Law or the later Coleridge and Schelling, a true renewal of Christianity had to rest on twin poles: it must be of absolute universal validity and it must be entirely self-authenticating, nothing less would do.

For the renewal of Christianity and the young Christian Community a century later, it was now essential that Böhme transmitted a philosophy that is entirely centred on the indwelling of Christ in the soul, that this is a new birth, *and* that the sacrament of the Eucharist is placed at the heart of life.

Both Hermann Beckh and Rudolf Steiner — as well as Goethe, Hegel and Schelling — were very aware that Böhme's 'open gate' to the spirit in the world and the human soul led from the beginning in 1612, then through the 1618 works *The Three Principles* and *The Threefold Life of Man* and all the later works, to an analysis of *the spiritual ground of substance*. It is precisely this which is vital for a balanced approach not only to Beckh's *Alchymie*, but also to the course of his publications as a whole.

Overall it is fair to say, I believe, that these traditions have a beating heart, one that has never stopped. This is the perception, often directly experienced, that matter is not a fixed and circumscribed *noun*, a 'substantive', but the arena of spiritual forces, beings or hierarchies that can be presented as *verbs in action*. From the very beginning of his lectures and publications on the origin of speech in 1921, Professor Beckh consistently brought his professorial knowledge of Tibetan, Sanskrit and Avestan to bear on this insight.[7] Ten years later, age 56, *Alchymie* became the subtitle of *Vom Geheimnis der Stoffeswelt* — 'On the Mystery of the World of Substance'. Now celebrating at the altars of The Christian Community with profoundly deepened spiritual knowledge, the Reverend Professor Beckh could address the two absolutely central questions: how far can we understand Earthly substances? How might the 'Reformation Reformed' now consider the Eucharist? While the answers to these questions pre-eminently depended on Rudolf Steiner, they also touched on the replies of the older Rosicrucians and alchymists enlightened by Jakob Böhme's thinking.

*

The spiritual ground of substance, the fundamental topic in *Alchymie*, was presented to Jakob Böhme as the total interplay of seven 'Qualities' (*Qualitäten*) or 'Fountain-spirits' (*Quellen-geister / Quellen*). Böhme continually wrestled between 1612 and 1624 to find an appropriate terminology for each of these but the overall understanding remained essentially unchanged. What is meant by 'interplay' we shall consider later, but one should immediately grasp that it is the *totality of the dynamic process* that requires attention rather than the individual forms. Nevertheless, the forms still have to be taken one by one as a scaffolding for the whole, although the division is somewhat artificial.

Quality 1: 'Astringent' — this is the primal centripetal dynamic or 'indrawing'. It strives to pull all into itself, to establish definition, to hold in. It is related to the Paracelsan understanding of *Sal* (salt) as mass, and also to Paracelsan ash. In the *Aurora* Böhme uses the alchemical term 'Salitter'. It is Saturnian, entropic, and is represented by the sound 'ma'. Coleridge, having read and copiously annotated his copy of Böhme's works,[8] decided on 'defining form'.

Quality 2: 'Bitter' — the polar complementary opposite of the astringent quality. It is that which fundamentally resists definition and fixation. It is centrifugal, striving for liberty, the expression of Divine freedom or 'Lubet'. This is related to Paracelsus' Mercury and ideas of unavoidable growth and change. It is represented by the syllable 'ku' and understood by Coleridge as 'Free Life'. In the *Mysterium Magnum* (1623) it is even presented as 'the disobedient son'.

Quality 3: 'Bitter sting' or 'Compunction' or 'Turba'. Since the 'first' two qualities are an irreconcilable polarity (reminiscent of Yin and Yang) and are totally interpenetrating, the result is an *intensifying* 'wheel' as the two dynamics struggle increasingly for dominance. This is *der Stachel*: the sting, thorn or perhaps goad, the driving force. Böhme sometimes called it '*Salfur*', with *Sal* representing Quality 1 and *Fur* (Fire) Quality 2. It is found in the intense syllable /ʁiː/ where /ʁ/ represents the uvular r of seventeenth century East Silesian. Here the polarity is expressed by /ʁ/ an 'astringent' low sound right at the back of the mouth and the high front vowel /iː/. As an escalation of opposed forces the bitter sting has been related to Mars: heat and movement are generated here, accompanied by a dull, formless noise *'pochen'*: knocking, tapping, thumping.

Quality 4: The 'Fire-crack' or *'Blitz'* or 'Salnitral flagrat'. It will be readily understood that the only possible result of *der Stachel* is some kind of explosion (terrifyingly conveyed in Gustav Holst's 'Mars'). Böhme relates this to the crack of lightning that attempts to solve or release the polarity of natural forces in earth and cloud, and also to his experience of gunpowder (where 'Salniter' is an ingredient) during the early years of the Thirty Years War in Silesia. The intensifying, restless 'Turba' is rent apart and Qualities 1–3 sizzle back to a state of lower energy: the sound is /ʊs/.

Qualities 1–4 in their dynamic process formed for Jakob Böhme what he called 'the First Principle': an analysis of energy, especially as warmth, which underlies the spiritual constitution (or hypostasis / substance) of the Divine Nature or Pleroma: a kind of *Urgrund*. The Fall of Lucifer has kindled the First Principle (Zeal of God) into his own dwelling-place, and humanity is quite able to do the same as the four Qualities are also constitutive of human nature. In other words, as the existentialist theologians at Beckh's time and William Blake earlier realized, the unregenerate Mind will become caught in hopeless paradoxes and polarities, circling feverishly, meeting one desperate crisis after another. Böhme combined the four speech sounds to find a name or token for this dark world of blind drives: *Marcurius* – Mercury in its dark side as a deadly poison, hegemon of the underworld, patron saint of trade and commerce, taken up by Milton as 'darkness visible'.[9]

Quality 4: yet the *Blitz* (a bolt of lightning) can also bring *light* into the darkness of subconscious forces, sub-earthly energies, with the potential to change all things in heaven and earth. The fourth Quality is twofold: a closed door leading back to the unchanged given Turba, or the gate to spiritual reformation, the start of a new life. This 'gate' is the Son of God, the Christ, and in Böhme's experience what is called for (*ecclesia*) is an acceptance of the light of Christ through the *Gelassenheit* of earlier Pietism, a quiet, peaceful resignation of the 'lower' egotistic 'I-am' to the spiritual foundation of the world, the divine I AM. As a Lutheran, Böhme wanted to emphasize that the transfiguration of Qualities through the Divine Light of Christ brings something *entirely new*: an entirely new state of being which he consequently called 'the

Second Principle'. Qualities 1–3 become transfigured, utterly metamorphosed into Qualities 5–7. In *Alchymie*, Beckh is quite right to
observe that, for the philosophical alchemist, Christ works as the
'Light-tincture' the agent of metamorphosis, although the term is not
very common in Böhme.

Quality 5: *die Temperatur*, or 'Tincture': light revealed in a 'sweet water'
as a harmony of colours in movement, symbolized by *the rainbow*. Here
the furious antagonism of the Turba is resolved into *a light-filled balance* of
phenomena where dark energies reappear now transfigured as an ever-
shifting panorama of interweaving colours. Within The Christian
Community and anthroposophy, Hermann Beckh finds a close analogy
with Rudolf Steiner's explication of self-conscious thinking (Böhme's
Blitz) progressing to Imagination, a reformed astrality both in Spirit-self
and the future incarnation of the Earth in the Jupiter state.

Quality 6: Tone and Speech. In the First Principle the 'bitter' Quality
expresses the Faustian unclear and unconscious urge to freedom,
change and growth. This is metamorphosed with the Revelation of
Christ into, successively, tones, music and speech. What 'initially' (but
see below) was manifest as *Pochen* (I am also reminded of Stravinsky's
'The Rite of Spring') becomes ultimately revealed as meaningful language. Again, Hermann Beckh finds parallels with the anthroposophical understanding of Inspiration, Life-spirit and the future
Venus state. However, it is precisely because speech is grounded in the
Qualities that Böhme had the direct experience of *Natursprache* or 'the
language of Nature'.[10]

Quality 7: The *Jungfrau Sophia*. The process of the Divine Will and
Logos entering into manifestation 'culminates' in the first Quality
(centripetal / astringent) becoming transfigured into a new Substance,
best understood as Hypostasis: compare also the clarified discovery in
Steiner's *The Philosophy of Freedom* and the earlier epistemological
works that in a natural-supernatural process, spiritual-physical, Being
is inseparable from the function of clear cognition and the work of
language. The initial Salitter finds fulfilment in establishing identity:
distinct substance and distinct concept. While there are obvious connections with the anthroposophical view of Intuition, Spirit-man and
the Vulcan state, still more pressing here is the notion, eloquently
discussed by Sergei Prokofieff in *Anthroposophy and The Philosophy of
Freedom*, that through Christ, consubstantial with the I AM, the substance or hypostasis of the resurrection body is created, in seed form,
through moral intuition.[11] Here we finally reach Hermann Beckh's

theme in *Alchymy,* whether portrayed as 'the philosopher's stone' (with reference to the first German edition of Steiner's *Occult Science,* the 'terra lucida' of Paradise, the 'Stone of the Wise' or the jewels of the New Jerusalem.

Broadly speaking, the eighteenth century transmission of Böhme, including in Britain the diluting influence of John Pordage, fell prey to setting out the Qualities as separate entities. This is almost certainly unavoidable, as above, but it is far better to grasp the unity of the whole process. From the start, Jakob Böhme took over from the Paracelsists and Raymond Lull the notion of *devictio,* 'overcoming'. In the *Aurora* he explains that it is almost impossible to perceive the whole circulation, the 'wheel' of Qualities in their rapid motion. Nevertheless he also explains that each form is within every other and each distinguishable manifestation only appears when one temporarily 'triumphs' over the others. This is the Paracelsan *devictio*—today one can imagine carbon appearing as wood-ash, graphite or diamond, but the idea was also a prompt for Goethe's natural science. The archetypal plant could appear as leaf, blossom or seed with seven 'stages' altogether: stem, node, leaf, corolla, calyx, pistil/ anther, and seed depending on which quality 'triumphs' (the technical term) at any one time. The value of *devictio* as a way of beholding phenomena is still high today. At any one time, once again, one's personality will manifest in one form or another; a concept will have a triumphing meaning yet 'contain' other latent possibilities which may emerge; in fact any phenomenon empirical, psychological or spiritual should be seen as mutable, one quality may be dominant at one time yet others are waiting to emerge. With great clarity and considerable linguistic prowess, Böhme saw that the pleroma of qualities was not only an arena of rapid change, but also a *Lieberspiel* — a game or sport where the Qualities lovingly 'tussle' or 'wrestle'[12] with each other, each within each, to attain a temporary 'triumph' before subsiding and moving on to further metamorphoses. We rise from observing forms to perceiving forms in holistic movement.

The whole dynamic structure of Böhme's Qualities is, in fact, *a seven-fold chiasm* within a circulation where the 'wheel' of metamorphosis is a lemniscate *in time* not in place, symbolized by the seven candles on the altar or the Jewish menorah. While it is obvious that Steiner's sevenfold chiasmic structure of world and human evolution re-expresses Böhme's vision (within a Rosicrucian tradition)—also meticulously analysed by Alan Stott in the sentence structures throughout *The Philosophy of Freedom*[13]—it is less well appreciated that Böhme's analysis of Qualities 4–7 also correlates quite closely with Steiner's presentation of the four ethers as discussed by Hermann Beckh:

The Sal-nitral flagrat or *Blitz*	→	The warmth-ether underlying the ego and the blood
The Tincture or Light-tincture	→	The light-ether
Tone, Music, Speech	→	The chemical / sound-ether
The Jungfrau Sophia	→	The life-ether

Consequently, looking at Böhme's works and the Kabbalistic tradition of the Sephiroth, it becomes possible to identify the often unspoken principle lying within or behind the chiasmic process of the Qualities. In short, Hermann Beckh would have been one of the first to agree that the *devictio* displayed in the whole process of seven forms is no less than the progressive manifestation of the I AM revealed as the hypostasis of world and human nature. *We have, in fact, seven forms of the I AM,* the 'last' of which Beckh celebrates in this small book on Alchymie: the new *I-substance* of the resurrection body and the formation of the New Jerusalem.

It is this *World-Passover* which Professor Hermann Beckh brings back to The Christian Community and to anthroposophy as he investigates the Gospels of Mark and John, Richard Wagner's *Parsifal*, and finally *Alchymie*. For the twenty-first century we can now approach Jakob Böhme, philosophical alchemy and the heart of Christianity as the transfiguring Passover of the I AM in humanity and the substance of the Earth. It is only natural, however, that we scarcely have the vocabulary for this: even in 1944 Carl G. Jung was wrestling with language to express his view of the Philosopher's Stone just as an image or icon of the *integration* of the human psyche with the form of the fourth as the disobedient son. Compared to this, Hermann Beckh and Rudolf Steiner were entering dimensions that were so much more in advance where we are summoned to relate anthroposophical terms to the earlier language of Paracelsus and Jakob Böhme. Beckh, more than anyone else at the time, strove with immense erudition and sensitivity to establish this call to the future: how *will we* understand that natural substances, matter, and the experiences of the human soul are both equally transformations of the divine I AM slumbering in the cosmos and awakened at the eucharist?

Neil Franklin

Translator's note

Hermann Beckh's (1875–1937) use of the archaic form '*Alchymie*' and '*Chymie*' and their derivatives has been preserved here in their English equivalents. The author intends to link to the genuine practitioners and exponents of the tradition. He would no doubt have been interested in more recent researchers, nevertheless Beckh's early study on alchymy is subject to no sell-by date. Though the subject, Beckh explicitly points out, does not lend itself to 'book-knowledge', in a lecturing style he nevertheless allows himself to introduce the subject. The result is a further contribution to his substantial studies on the Gospels of Mark, and in particular of John (also pub. 1930), referred to in Chapter 5 as the author's book on John's Gospel. This present 'introduction', *Alchymy*, however, can also serve as a way into the author's other studies in spirituality, world-religions, language and music.

The Earth, along with the Sun and other planets have been capitalized, for they are proper names, and other technical terms such as Imagination, Inspiration and Intuition, stages of higher cognition used in anthroposophy. *Das Ich* is rendered the 'I', with inverted commas because in English it is unusual as a noun, and also, though less frequently, rendered as 'the ego' — admittedly this is another foreign word that is frequently associated with specific psychological meanings not specifically intended by the author. Professor Beckh is in accord with the emphasis ascribed to this human member in anthroposophy, or 'spiritual science'. In this area, or rather activity — as justified in the Translator's Note to the author's book on Mark's Gospel (MG) — I have most frequently translated *Geheimnis* as 'mystery' as more accurate today than 'secret', and *Wandlung*, and similar words, occasionally as 'metamorphosis' from the Greek, rather than 'transformation' from the Latin. In both cases, the aim of accuracy in translation also includes the attempt to surmount any hint of something taking place automatically. Again, verbal forms rather than nouns often work best in English. Motivation is ever the expectation of all educators, trying to stimulate the genuine article — self-knowledge, something beyond 'self-development' and the like. Love, we are told, starts with interest. That 'me' may become 'I' is one way of expressing Beckh's overriding concern.

Beckh's occasionally overlong sentences have been broken up. Editorial additions appear in [ ]. The bibliographical details have been updated where known. Many texts by Rudolf Steiner are available online: www.rsarchive.org. 'GA' numbers refer to the *Gesamtausgabe*, the Collected Works. It may be worth noting that Friedrich Benesch's *Apocalypse: The Transformation of the Earth, an esoteric Mineralogy*, tr. Joseph Bailey, has been published by Lindisfarne Books, Great Barringon 2015. Benesch was a successor of Beckh at the Priests' Seminary, Stuttgart.

My grateful thanks to help in this translation go to my wife Maren, who is bi-lingual. Special thanks go to Neil Franklin, Ph.D., scholar of Boehme and Blake, for his Introduction, editorial help, snippets of expert knowledge, and very much more.

Alan Stott
Epiphany 2015

I know not whether anyone ever truly understood the rocks and stars, but any such must have been a sublime being.
 Novalis. *The Novices of Sais*, from Chap. 4.

In vain we ask, with yearning fond,
The form of that which lies beyond:
Interrogate them, as we will,
The stars on high are silent still;
Silent the graves, nor make reply
The dearest lips therein that lie.
 Goethe, from *Symbolum*

The world appears round as a sphere,
That's why away it will pass,
The City of God is a cube,
That's why forever it stands fast.
 Angelus Silesius

I.

Alchymy and Man's Past:
Rosicrucianism, the Virginal Earth, the Philosopher's Stone

Through all the ancient accounts of humanity, through legends, poetry and fairy-tales, through the great sacred texts themselves, there runs a singing and relating of a virginal secret of the world, ultimately of the material world. This secret, or mystery, of the material world, which has its spiritual home in earlier times, especially in Egypt, was sought in the Middle Ages and the beginning of modern times. In their way the alchemists called it 'virginal earth', *terra sancta* 'sacred earth', and '*materia benedicta*', or in the language of the Gospel, 'the treasure in the field' [to obtain which a man 'sells all he has and buys that field', Matt. 13:44]. The starting point of their 'chymical processes' was for them the *prima materia*, the 'first' or original matter, through which they intended to elevate and ennoble the material and transform base metal or stones into noble metals or stones, trying to obtain the secrets of gold and precious stones. What they found or sought also included the essence of the 'elixir' that purifies and heals, enlivens and rejuvenates human nature, what they then called the 'philosopher's stone', *lapis philosophorum,* the 'stone' or 'waterstone of the wise'.[14]

These attempts directed towards the 'finding of the philosopher's stone' of the early alchemists, however we evaluate their factual backgrounds and relationship to reality, led to all kinds of discoveries in natural science; out of the 'chymistry' of that time, purely historically and factually, has come the chemistry of today. Its name bears its country of origin, which, as we say, was once the home of its spiritual predecessor: *chemi, chemet* was the ancient local name in Egypt.

The words of the mystic Angelus Silesius also point in the direction of the Mysteries touched on here:

The finest thing in all the world
Is the pure virginal Earth;

One says, that out of it
The Child of the Wise will be made.
[*Cherubinischer Wandersmann*. (C.W.) Book 1, 147.]

Here the 'virginal earth' is the starting point of the '*philosopher's stone*
(Stein der Weisen—*stone of the wise*)' the '*child of the wise* (Kind der
Weisen)' which is the end product of the chymical process. This
'philosopher's stone', this end result of the chymical process, was also
called the *tincture*. In this tincture the power was embodied to transform base metal, especially lead or quicksilver, into noble metals, into
silver and gold. The silver-producing tincture, also called 'tincture of
the Moon', is described as shining grey or white; the gold-producing
'tincture of the Sun', an intensive red powder of a unique, layered slate-
like, flaking structure. In the text *Das Geheimnis von dem Salz* by
Friedrich Christof Oetinger,[15] we find the following (para. 68, p. 126f.):

> The tincture *solis* is carmine-scarlet coloured, deep ruby red comparable
> to the highly shining polished gold, the clear shining of the Sun, the rose
> colour of the blood, and is constant in colour and tincture, so that it gives a
> majestic sheen.

The secret of the 'red tincture' repeatedly lights up in alchymical and
Rosicrucian writings of the Middle Ages and right into modern times.
The essence of 'tingeing', or colouring—*tincture* from Lat. *tingere* 'to
colour'—is that a proportionally small amount of the relevant substance given to the base metal is supposed to transform large quantities
of it; for us today the quantities expressing proportions as given by the
alchemists appear fantastic.

Certainly, with the 'chymical secrets' touched on here, it does not
only concern 'producing gold'. During the course of our observations it
will become increasingly clear how the essence of the 'chymical', in
contrast to 'chemical', has to be sought. Here one cannot remain as in
chemistry with the outer material. One has to recognize how the secret
of the material itself is woven into higher cosmic and human contexts,
how all 'maya' [illusion] of the material originates in the reality of the
spiritual supersensory realm. *True alchymy begins in the human being and
ends in the material world.* It carries within itself the secret of metamorphosis, the transformation or transubstantiation of the earthly element.
This change, working from the spiritual element, takes place in the
human being himself, at first invisibly and then more and more visibly,
taking hold of earthly matter. That which in the writings of the
alchymists and Rosicrucians can be found or guessed as verities leads

ultimately into the Christian Mystery of the Resurrection. The alchymists themselves everywhere emphasize the connection of their 'chymical secrets' with the Christian Mysteries, of the 'philosopher's stone' with Christ as cornerstone (Luke 20:17). Angelus Silesius says:

> Your stone, chymist, is nothing;
> The cornerstone that I mean
> Is my gold tincture,
> Is the stone of all the philosophers.
> [C. W. Book 1, 280]

For him the change of matter becomes the picture or parable of higher metamorphosis and purification processes in the human being:

> Observe the tincturing,
> Then you see how beautifully and free
> How your redemption and
> Your deification will be.
> [C. W. Book 1, 258]

Jakob Böhme coins his obscure words in profound cosmic and cosmogonic visions and he likes to draw on chymical pictures and ways of expression. He appeals to the alchemists in his writing *De incarnatione Verbi* [1620] 'of the Word that became flesh': 'let this be revealed to you, you seekers of metallic tincture: if you want to find the *Lapidem Philosophorum*, then turn to the new birth in Christ' [Chapter 4, para 10].

Chymical expressions, such as, 'philosopher's stone' (or 'stone of the wise') and 'tincture' appear in earlier literature, frequently as pictures where purification and spiritualization of the earthly element and the human being is discussed. In linguistic use, furthermore, these two expressions do not always mean the same. The 'philosopher's stone' is usually the transformed 'tincture', the end product of the 'chymical process'. Sometimes, however, it is also the initial substance, the *prima materia*, the starting point of the chymical process, the 'virginal earth', the mystery-woven substance governing super-materially in matter that is hidden in the human being and in the Earth. Jakob Böhme in whose chymical vocabulary the 'tincture' plays such an important role, uses this word not only in the sense of the metal-transforming substance, but somehow connects it with the 'virginal mystery of the world of matter', in such a way that he means by it more the super-sensory, super-material side, the *living etheric side* of this Mystery, as we can also say, than that initial product of the chymical process lying more in the physical-material realm.

The way Böhme uses the word 'tincture' allows us think of the connection, so important to the alchymists, of the *life-ether* as the highest of the four kinds of ether and the firm earthly matter as the lowest of the elements. These are not the 'elements' of today's chemistry. Rather what is meant here is what the chemist and physicist would call the 'aggregate condition of matter'. This mystery of the life-ether, of life itself, is most intimately related to the mysteries of alchymy. The details of the kinds of ether are explained in Dr Günther Wachsmuth's book on the *The Etheric Formative Forces in Cosmos, Earth and Man*.[16] On the one hand, there are the three kinds of ether, the warmth-ether, the light-ether and the chemical-, or sound-ether. These are not perceptible to the sensory eye and to science researching in the sensory realm. However, they are revealed in the sensory realm through their effects — for example, the chemical-ether, in the realm of all chemical processes. The mystery of the life-ether, though, lies still one level higher and cannot be laid hold of in such a way as the mystery of the three other kinds of ether that can be laid hold of in a certain way. Only when we are able to raise ourselves from the realm of chemistry to that other *chymical* realm, for humanity today hidden under the veil of the secrets of nature, can we approach the mysteries of this highest ether, and with it to the mystery of the earthly element, to the actual mystery of matter.[17]

All this is deeply grounded in the primal history of mankind. Spiritual science shows us how in the life-ether, bound with the chemical-ether, or sound-ether, lies the higher element of life lost to humanity in the Fall of Man. The *Tree of Life* was lost when primal humanity was expelled from Paradise. Therewith the higher, chymical-magical full power over the earthly element was also lost. And so for people today a veil appears to cover the mystery of alchymy as a direct consequence of the Fall of Man. Caught in the net of consequences, the human being is caught in the results of the cause, displaced from mastering it. Those wielding powers in the lower material world have been able at one time in the realm of causes to usurp for themselves the power reserved for the human 'I'. For this whole cosmic and human context, in the whole mystery of the Fall of Man and of the loss of certain higher knowledge and the powers it brought about, Jakob Böhme allows us a glimpse in the way he speaks about *tincture*:

Man was created to be a Lord of Tincture, who was to be subject to him, but he became her servant, became a stranger. So then he sought only for gold and found earth; consequently, by losing the Spirit and going with *his* spirit into existence [*Wesenheit*, literally 'being-ness'], existence captured him, embraced by death. The tincture of earth lies sealed in wrath, right up to the judgement of God; and the human spirit also lies sealed in the wrath of God, so he went his way in order to be [re-]born in God (*De incarnatione Verbi*).[18]

Jakob Böhme's obscure words indicate the reason why the human spirit, despite all the many aspects of natural scientific knowledge, is displaced so far from the actual mystery of nature, and why the whole realm is covered by a thick veil, so that all discussion of alchymy today [written 1931] is regarded almost as fantastic error or worse.

In the pictures of the Egyptian religion and of spiritual science [anthroposophy] Isis was the Queen of the Stars and Mother of the Earth, the Governess of the Life-ether of the stars and of the element of earth. Osiris was the cosmic Word, the Lord of the sound-ether and of the element of water. Isis belonged to the Egyptian earth, Osiris to the Nile. In this sense, we can say the 'veil of Isis', which is a veil of stars and a veil of matter, covers the questionable realm for people today. Retreating in reverence before this veil, the spirit of poetry in Goethe coined in his Masonic poem '*Symbolum*', so deeply inspired by the cosmic mystery, the verse [in this poetic version by Arthur James Lockhart, *Ehrfurcht* 'devotion' is translated 'yearning'. See below]:

> In vain we ask, with yearning fond,
> The form of that which lies beyond:
> Interrogate them, as we will,
> The stars on high are silent still;
> Silent the graves, nor make reply
> The dearest lips therein that lie.

In his *Fragments* (ed. Kamnitzer 2152) Novalis speaks programmatically of 'mysticism of nature', of Isis, of the 'Virgin and Veil', of the 'mysterious dealing of natural science'. His poetic prose work *The Novices of Sais* is completely filled with the scent of the virginal mysteries of nature, of the 'longing for the eternal Virgin' — as Isis is also named there. Chapter One ends:

> ... if no mere mortal can lift the veil obscuring every inscription that lies yonder; then we must all strive towards immortality; he who does not seek to lift the veil is no true Saisian novice.

* * *

Like Jakob Böhme speaking of 'tincture', Novalis speaks of the 'philosopher's stone' in a still completely super-material, etheric-spiritualized sense. In an initially surprising, ungraspable manner for a thinking oriented to Kant's *Critique of Pure Reason*, Novalis relates the philosopher's stone to the *mystery of space and time*; he calls it 'invisible visible material', which is 'everywhere and nowhere[19], everything and nothing', and throws out the question, whether there is a corresponding possibility also in relation to time (Fragment 613. Wood 1035):

> Isn't there a *faculty* in us playing the same role here as the *heavenly firmament* does outside of us? — the *ether* — that invisible visible matter, the philosopher's stone — which is everywhere and nowhere, everything and nothing — We call it *instinct* or genius — It is everywhere *antecedent*. It is the *fullness of the future* — the *fullness of the ages* in general — becoming for time, what the philosopher's stone is for space ...

For an active thinking, activated by the 'I' — already anticipated by Novalis for all transformation of that which is earthly, decisively important for all high alchymy — space and time no longer remain the abstract 'forms of understanding' in the sense of Kantian philosophy. There they become living revelations of being, still carrying within essentially all the divine 'active forces and seed', the seed of all becoming in the fashioning of matter. The 'philosopher's stone' is to be sought in the deepest, most esoteric sense at that point where the super-spatial and the super-temporal manifest within existence in space and time; space and time go over into the super spatial and temporal sphere. The former is the viewpoint of the past, the latter the future viewpoint, the alchymy. Before us we see a cosmically profound, 'chymical', future-meaning of Christianity, still very distant from every Christian confession, a viewpoint prepared today in anthroposophy for humanity. This viewpoint, ahead of a whole future development of human thinking, is once again expressed in words by Novalis (Fragment 1719, ed. Kamnitz; Wood 1095), the profound cosmic sense of which human thinking today can hardly grasp:

> The opinion concerning the negativity of Christianity is excellent. Christianity thereby becomes elevated to the level of a foundation — the projecting forces for a new edifice of the world and humanity — to a genuine heavenly firmament — to a living moral space.
>   This wonderfully relates to my ideas regarding the hitherto mis-

understood nature of *space* and *time*, whose personality and archetypal force have now become indescribably illuminating to me. The activity of *space* and *time* is the force of creation, and their relations are the hinges of the world.

Absolute abstraction—annihilation of the present,—apotheosis of the future, of this veritable better world: all belong to the inner core of Christianity—and thereby unite it with the religion of the ancient world, with the divinity of the ancients with the restoration of antiquity, as its second principal wing.—And like the body of an angel, both hold the universe in eternal suspense—in an everlasting enjoyment of *space* and *time*.

Already at this point in the discussion we can sense how the 'chymical' future perspective on Christianity given here by Novalis meets the Johannine apocalyptic vision of the 'New Jerusalem', of the chymically transformed Earth of the future and its revelation of the mystery of space enclosed in its symbol of a cube (Rev. 21:16). Something like the inner progress from the abstract imagination of space, in Kant's view, to the living revelation of space in the anthroposophical view, becomes visible here. Rudolf Steiner leads us nearer to understand all these connections, first pointed out by Novalis, when discussing the apocalyptic seals and pictures, Berlin 1907.[*] He explains the seventh seal ('of the Holy Grail') that contains the symbol of the cube, with reference to Rev. 21:16:

> The cube represents the spatial world not yet penetrated by any physical being and by no physical event. It is space, not simply emptiness, but the carrier that still bears invisibly in itself the seed of everything physical. Out of it there precipitates, as it were, the whole physical world as salt precipitates out of the still translucent solution.

It is of deepest significance for the whole problem of alchymy, how here Rudolf Steiner helps us to understand the mystery of space revealed in the three dimensions of the cube. Salt (crystalizing into the cube) is connected to this, which recalls Oetinger's treatise mentioned above, where he explains the 'mystery of the salt' as that of the philosopher's stone.

Steiner first uses the expression 'philosopher's stone' itself when, in the first lecture-cycle (*At the Gates of Spiritual Science*. Stuttgart, 22 Aug.–4 Sept. 1906. GA 95, Lecture 13, on 'pranayama'), he speaks of 'yoga-breathing'. He speaks of the breathing exercises and refinement of the

---

[*] GA 284, p. 94. See also the lecture, Stuttgart, 16 Sept. 1907 in GA 101 — *Tr. note.*

breathing process in the schooling of Indian yoga. There he touches on certain mysteries of carbon dioxide, showing how in controlling the breath the human being retains elements of carbon dioxide, and similar to the plant, how CO_2, otherwise breathed out by human beings, is breathed in somewhat like the plant, and is used to build a refined corporeality. The transformation of carbon into the translucent carbon crystal, the *diamond*, is used as a comparison. 'Then,' Steiner says at this point, 'he has found the philosopher's stone, he transforms his whole body into the philosopher's stone.'[20]

Steiner often emphasized that in the Rosicrucian schooling, in the Western meditation schooling proceeding from thinking, the same process of the transformation of breathing takes place. This appears in an especially remarkable way in the lecture-course on agriculture, where carbon is presented as the 'philosopher's stone', which, of course, has to be taken with a pinch of salt. The relationship of meditation to the process of breathing in the Eastern schooling is a direct one, in the Western indirect. On the connection of the process of meditation with the process of breathing, see *Anthroposophie*: Dornach 1927, p. 88.[21] In the first German edition of the book *Esoteric Science* [1910, p. 352] Steiner still used for the rhythmicizing of the breath in the Rosicrucian schooling: 'working with the philosopher's stone'. The starting point of chymical processes, which for humanity today is still deeply veiled in mysteries, is everywhere closer to us than we think. In the mystery of breathing, in the mystery of carbon to which it is connected, this process could somehow be laid hold of in one's own body. Alchymy begins in the human being and ends in the realm of matter.

Where Imagination, Inspiration and Intuition as the three levels of the path of [cognitive] knowledge are differentiated, the work with the 'philosopher's stone' meant here belongs to the latter, the level of Intuition. Herein we touch the innermost mystery of the physical realm and of its transformation, which at the same time is the *Mystery of Resurrection*. We are close to this mystery of the resurrection, not where the supersensory essence, the element overcoming death in the etheric or astral, can already be found, but only where it can also be found in the physical. In the lecture cycle *From Jesus to Christ* (Karlsruhe, 5–14 October 1911. GA 131, Lectures 6–8), Steiner discusses this super-sensory-physical as the 'phantom' of the resurrection body, which as such is clearly different from the ether-body. As the etheric element relates to the earthly plant-element, so the phantom-forces of the supersensory-physical relate to the forces of the crystals, the archetypal mineral element of the cosmos. The 'phantom-forces' once existed during the primeval, Ancient Saturn conditions of the human being. Because of the Fall of Man they were increasingly used up. The phantom-forces, newly enlivened through the power of Christ, formed the substance of the Resurrection Body, which, as the primal cell of a new Earth and a new Humanity, rose out of the grave of Golgotha. In the above-mentioned lecture-cycle [GA 131], Steiner even points towards the context of the realm of facts lying behind this 'resurrection phantom', with the realm of alchemy and the 'philosopher's stone':

The alchemists have always emphasized that the human body in truth consists of the same substance of which the *completely transparent, crystal bright 'philosopher's stone'* consists [Lecture 6].

For this supersensory-physical element related to the crystal forces of the cosmos — not what presents itself as 'body' to sensory appearance, to outer sensory perception — is in truth the 'physical body' of the human being, in the sense of higher spiritual knowledge.

Buddha also knew something of these things, of an 'octahedral secret of the inner diamond' and its context with the supersensory physical. In his description of the path of meditation in the *Dīghanikāya*, he speaks of achieving 'body-free knowing', of wresting a finer spiritual body out of the physical corporeality. He speaks in such a way that he sees before him the composition of that 'inner supersensory corporeality' and its relationship to the consciousness-soul in the picture of a 'pure, spotless eight-sided precious stone'[22] through which a coloured thread is pulled. The 'eight-sided precious stone' is the diamond crystalizing into the octahedron, whose play of colour (the 'coloured thread') then appears as a picture of higher revelation of consciousness (*cf.* the author's book on *Buddha und seine Lehre*. 185f. [*Buddha's Life and Teaching*, Temple Lodge, 2019]). We also find with Buddha that in breathing lie the 'formative forces of the body' (*kāyasaṃskāra, kāyasaṇkhāra*). These occasional echoes in Buddha in what is still retained from later ages of Indian wisdom appear to us all the more remarkable, considering the otherwise diminishing awareness of alchemy as well as the astrology connected to it. Reading between the lines of Buddhist traditional texts, mysteries of the zodiac as well as planetary wisdom may still be discovered in which genuine primal wisdom is contained, whereas what has been handed down as 'Indian astrology' from later times, while interesting, bears marks of decadence and a gypsy-like character, primarily showing foreign, mainly Greek, influences.

In connection with the chymical secrets of metamorphosis, of the 'inner diamond' and its relationship to the 'philosopher's stone', we are already reminded of the 'Earth of light' of the Manicheans, which Albert Steffen describes in his book *Mani*.[23] This *terra lucida*, this 'Earth of light', 'possesses a spiritual kernel and an etheric envelope'. [Ibid., 50] In the lecture-course on Christian Rosenkreutz (Neuchâtel. 27 Sept. 1911. GA 130), Rudolf Steiner explains how especially in the border realm between the physical and the etheric the substance can be found which the Rosicrucians sought as the supersensory substance of their 'philosopher's stone'. The supersensory-physical connects here with the etheric realm, with the mystery of the higher kinds of ether.

> Clairvoyantly to visualize this substance (says Steiner, *op. cit.*) was the aim of the Rosicrucians. The preparation for beholding this substance was for them a moral deed ... They found this in the world and the human being. Outside the human being, they venerated this substance as the garment of the cosmos. In the human being, they saw it arising when harmony arises between thinking and the will.

Rudolf Steiner always emphasized the meaningful connections between Rosicrucianism and the teaching of Mani, the inner connection of the two great initiates Christian Rosenkreutz and Mani — separated on Earth by a millennium. In Steffen (p. 50) we find the following concerning the *Lichterde*, the 'Earth of light':

> The *terra lucida* presents itself in its stages of becoming as *life* — life-breath, life-light, life-water, life-fire, and is a pre-earthly field of activity of divine-spiritual beings, who as aeons surround the God of Light. This earth of light, through the progressive influence of the aeons, little by little becomes the airy, liquid, firm earth, although the latter is at first enclosed in a skin-like membrane.

To Steffen's descriptions should be added that the name Mani itself, if we are allowed to take it in its Indian meaning of 'jewel, crystal', seems to indicate a connection with the 'crystal forces of the cosmos' we discuss here as the physical-supersensory primal substance of the 'philosopher's stone'. The similarity of *mani* to *man* 'thinking', *manas* 'spiritual primal substance' — unimportant for academic grammarians — can here be felt as significant.

The 'crystal forces of the cosmos' have been repeatedly mentioned here, indicating how the forces of space and of form, which are visibly revealed in the crystals of the mineral world, exist as a supersensory essence of forces and of light at a higher level of existence. In *The World of the Senses and the World of the Spirit* [Hannover, 27 Dec. 1911–1 Jan.

1912. GA 134, Lecture 4], Steiner describes that physical-mineral matter arises where the primal essence of the crystal bursts or disperses into the emptiness, into the 'virginal aspect of the world', here. (With the dispersing into the etheric and astral realm of the world there arise plant and animal matter.) Hereby, if something from the supersensory forming powers is as it were taken into the visible realm, then wonder can arise concerning the mineral crystals. The expression used here by Steiner of the 'virginal aspect of the world' for the mystery of the original spatial world not yet filled with matter, reminds us once more of the 'philosopher's stone', of Novalis and the 'virginal secret of the material world' that is encountered, as mentioned at the beginning of our studies. The connection always stressed in anthroposophy of the crystal forces, or the mineral in general, with the starry heaven – the upper planetary realm, beyond Saturn – in a more ancient esoteric tradition referred to as 'crystal spheres', is also significant for alchymy.

In this sense – also indicated by Novalis and Steiner – the 'philosopher's stone' would be a transcendental, archetypal nature or an archetypal crystal being that is poured over the emptiness of space as yet unfilled by matter. The spirit and the physical I and not-I meet in a mysterious manner: the power of the I is revealed in the primal cosmic nothingness.[24] Indian Sankhya philosophy approaches near to this sphere of cosmic thought with its *mūlaprākṛti* – specifically 'root nature' or 'primal nature', the '*Hyle*' of the Greeks – as the female principle of creation in contrast to *puruṣa* (purusha, emphasis on the first syllable) as the spiritual male principle. This Indian word *mūlaprākṛti*, taken purely linguistically, stands close to the alchymical expression *prima materia* 'initial materiality', although purely factually the alchymists' *prima materia* lay much deeper in matter.

In order to give a clear concept of this and at the same time a distinct example of the strange, riddling language of alchymical writings of past centuries, a passage may be quoted here from *Die Geheimen Figuren der Rosenkreutzer aus dem 16. und 17. Jahrhundert*:[25] according to Rudolf Steiner's indications in his lecture-course on Chr Rosenkreutz 1911 [GA 130. See Lecture 7, Neuchâtel, 27 Sept. 1911, in *Esoteric Christianity*, Rudolf Steiner Press, London, 2000], this book contains the renewal of the Christian-Rosicrucian impulse in eighteenth century):

> The *prima materia* has received its content from the *fiat* ['Let there be . . .'] of creation. And the *Word* proceeding from the *Father* through Whom all things were made, and the *Spirit* proceeding from both is the *divine-life*

creating Air. Consequently the Air amongst the elements makes all things alive. The Fire warms all things, the Water quickens, gives refreshment and supplies drink to everything; the Fire has also given birth to the Air and the Air blows up the Fire again that it can live; but the Air changed into Water becomes food for the Fire and in this element, Water and wetness of the ground, as in the slimy, fat wetness of the ground, the fire burns and the Earth as a container of nitrous salt [saltpetre] gives the nourishment for this, and in its belly all these elements live, for in this belly is the sulphuric nitrous salt 'salniter'[26] of nature, *the singular good thing that God has created in the visible world.*

The same *salt-mother of the elements* is the nitrous, aluminal, spiritual, oily, water, *salt-earth* or *crystal*, which nature has in its belly, a Son of the Suns, and a daughter of the Moon. It is a *hermaphrodite* whom the wind has carried in its belly; a *phoenix*, living in the fire, a *Pelican*, that with its own blood brings back to life its dead offspring; the young Icarus drowned in the Water, whose foster-mother is the Earth, the *Wind his mother*, the Fire his father, the Water his cleanser and drink, *a stone and no stone*, a Water and no Water, and yet a stone of living strength and Water of living power; a *sulphur*, a mercurius, *a salt which nature carries hidden in itself and has never been known or seen by anyone unwise.*

The attentive reader, reading between the lines, will discover in all the obscurity of the words many connections to what has been discussed here. Immediately in the Introduction to the above work, it says of the 'Prima Materia', p. 3 [p. 216]:

The beginning of the *subjectum*, the subject which is put into our hand by Nature in which the universal tincture of all metals, animals and plants is hidden is an undefined, raw body, has neither body nor form or an animal or a plant, but is at the beginning a rough, earthly, heavy, slimy, tough, foggy watery being, *with which Nature has ceased.* But when the enlightened human being takes up this matter, and tries to digest it, and purifies its thick, nebulous shadow that surrounds it, allowing what is hidden to crawl out, and through further sublimation coaxes out its inner soul that is hidden in it, then one finds what Nature has hidden in such a previously uncouth form, and what strength and *Magnalia* of the highest Creator has given and planted into this *Creatum*, creation [the secondary meaning of *Creatum* is 'that which has been prepared'].

As the further progress of this account will show more clearly, the expression here 'with which Nature has ceased' is especially impor-tant, in addition the reference to the 'digestion', to the whole mystery of the reception and metamorphosis of nourishment in the human body in the process of living. Many details still remain difficult to understand. Behind the whole search of the alchemists we dimly divine the ancient longing of humanity, which still speaks for us today in the joy of crystals, of gold and precious stones—even where it has become greed and pulled down the human being into dark abysses. The 'miraculous flower' in the fairy-tales, the 'precious pearl', the 'treasure in the field' [in the Gospels], are for us today the poetic or religious-pictorial expression of this longing. What was real in the alchemists' search we cannot decide today with evidential proof as long as the facts are missing. But the impartial examination of the '*Acta* of the Middle Ages' lead to assumptions of a factual background of alchemy, although amongst a hundred practitioners who boasted they were in command of the chymical art and in possession of chymical secrets there might have been only one single real initiate.

II.

Alchemy and Mankind in the Present: Chemistry and chymistry; The 'construction of the atom'; Salt, mercury, sulphur and the mystery of the threefold human being

At this point, where the discussion has been about the apparent achievements of alchymy stretching right into the realm of matter, however much we want to seek its actual essence in the spiritual realm, the observations have to concern themselves with all the objections that could be raised here from the side of natural science. Already in the nineteenth century people in professional scientific circles were, and are still today [written 1931], inclined to present alchemy as a proven falsehood or superstition that has been superseded, not even to allow it to exist as a question. Only with Karl Christoph Schmieder, whose *Geschichte der Alchemie* ['History of Alchemy', reprints and ebook available] appeared in 1832, the year of Goethe's death, do we find from an expert community a positive attitude, already expressively demonstrated at the beginning of the Foreword:

> People who want to question something that has been long established would meet justified disapproval; this would be the case for many people here. It is true, alchemy has lost its rights in the first instance; never-theless, if it is true it should have found a new justification, it would not suffer a loss to the demand for revision. Although centuries may have passed, its right cannot diminish, for truth is eternal and may not be condemned.

The spiritual touch perceptible in these sentences we miss completely in the book by the chemist Prof Dr Hermann Kopp, *Alchemie*, Heidelberg 1886, 2 vols, which appeared half a century later, although here too, with the negation of the fact of alchymy in the consciousness a certain tendency connects in the subconscious. As is not seldom the case with modern scholars, that which is *not clearly and consciously recognized* exercises a certain magical, sensational attraction on the soul.

We can observe how Kopp throughout his whole life's path is repeatedly led to the question of alchymy; his destiny is connected with it. When he then expresses himself positively on one of the historically famous transformations of metal—also mentioned in Schmieder's book, *op. cit.* p. 422—then, if we understand him correctly, there lies once again in such a confirmation basically the affirmation of alchymy, the reality he otherwise denies. Against the cases of thousands of frauds, through a single proven case of genuine transmutation the fact of alchymy itself would be proven.

In *Thomas von Aquino, Abhandlung über den Stein der Weisen* ['Thomas Aquinas: discussion on the philosopher's stone'],[27] the novelist and occultist Gutav Meyrink uncovers the relationship of this personality — a pupil of Albertus Magnus—to the alchymical strivings of his time. Meyrink points to a certain Adolf Helfferich, *Die neuere Naturwissenschaft, ihre Ergebnisse und Aussichten* ['The latest Natural Science: its Results and Prospects'] Trieste 1857, who takes a final positive stand in the nineteenth century for the factual existence of alchymy. Meyrink calls it a 'brilliant joke from the course of world-history', that this advocate of alchemical transformation of metals carried the same name as the one who, during the inflation after the Great War, brought about a reverse of metal transformation, that is, of gold into paper[-money].[28]

For the denial of the question of alchymy, as has been customary in academic circles for a long time, the assumptions increasingly fall away today. The system of Mendeleev, ordering the chemical elements according to their atomic weights, arrives at a scale of seven. A corresponding relationship occurs with the numerical order to the mutual relationship of the individual elements. This made us guess that those 'elements' are not the ultimate primal substance but the results of a higher synthesis. And through the recent researches of Rutherford — see, for example, Niels Bohr, *Über den Bau der Atome* ['The Structure of the Atom'][29]—this synthesis, the 'structure of the atom', is a proven fact. The aim of the present observations is not concerned with a critique or theoretical assessment of the theory of 'atoms', 'ions', and 'electrons', but only to look at the facts expressed in these formulations that the scientific community today assumes in discussing the theories in question.

Even for natural scientists themselves, the concepts 'atom', 'electron', and so on, are being increasingly stripped of their original, and therewith still material, notions. To them, the material increasingly becomes a system of forces, of 'energy', and behind this play of forces they begin to sense from afar the fact of 'consciousness' as the decisive ultimate reality of the 'mystery of the material world'. There is still but *one* step from this fact of 'consciousness' to that of 'spiritual beings', about which esoteric research and observation speaks.

To produce gold synthetically, even provisionally only in diminishing amounts, is taken as possible, according to Rutherford's results. Through this the *question* of alchymy is fundamentally affirmed today from the scientific side. Obviously, in its full sense it is not yet solved. The philosopher's stone has not been found. Only because people have not found it themselves, they will not admit that at some time – in another age and under other circumstances – some person could possibly have found it. Of course, with purely personal views of this kind, belonging to the transitory aspects of an age, nothing is decided concerning the facts themselves.

The Mystery of the Threefold Human Being

In his lecture-course on agriculture,[30] Rudolf Steiner said:

> Our chemistry speaks of the corpses of matter. It does not speak of real kinds of matter. These one has to get to know as living, sensing beings.

And he shows how [Lecture 3]

- the use and function of oxygen in the household of nature is related to the mysteries of the etheric, living element, and
- the use and function of nitrogen connects with the mysteries of the astral, sensing element – in this case, a real 'sensing of the Earth' – and
- the use and function of carbon dioxide joins with the mystery of the spiritual ego-nature
- and there is also the build-up of all plant and animal forms out of the cosmic spirit.

What has become dead through becoming and is researched in today's chemistry in its earthly manifestation has obviously to be preceded by a stage of becoming. In the hypothetical research of this stage of becoming, the natural-scientific notions of today reach as far as the conditions of the watery, flowing fire and gaseous forms that preceded the solid condition of the Earth's crust. A spiritual research that penetrates into the essentials cannot remain with such notions. Its strengthened thinking reaches far beyond the point reached here, from the material into the super-material, from the sensory into the super-sensory, from the physically dead into the etherically alive, and into the sensing of the astral element. And only by being able to find the ego-realm does it find tranquility in itself, beyond space and time. There the experience of thinking flows together with the primal processes of the world's becoming. The dynamic of thinking that in itself moves, strengthens and enlivens becomes cosmic drama, as it lives in Rudolf Steiner's *Esoteric Science, an Outline* [GA 13]. Reading between the lines it bears a chemistry of cosmic birth-processes, a *primal chemistry of that which lives*. And this is *alchymy*.

The obvious objection that the mystery of alchymy should thereby be remote from the present day, that it should disappear into a far past where we are no longer able to lay hold of it, does not meet the facts. But all those *ways of God into the realm of earthly matter*, which in *Esoteric Science* unroll before us in grandiose pictures of 'Ancient Saturn, Ancient Sun, Ancient Moon, and the Earth' are totally present in everything that lives, in human beings, plants and animals, still to be seen to this day. In the human being of water, the human being of air, and the human being of warmth that we carry within us in the circulation of fluids, in the breathing and the fire-element of the blood, there live connections of the primal etheric, of the primal astral and of the primal spiritual ego-nature (Sun, Moon, and Saturn) still present today. The clairvoyant, beholding these dramatic events as present actuality, translates this great cosmic panorama; we then participate in thinking it through in our own contemplations.

The contexts of the primal physical, of the primal Earth, essential for all alchymy as the basic *prima materia* ('first matter'), are furthermore revealed in all the processes of receiving nourishment and of digestion. Rudolf Steiner repeatedly spoke about these mysteries, still deeply veiled to people today, to farmers and theologians, natural scientists and physicians. Precisely here, as he has shown, lie all the mysteries of change, of transubstantiation—initially presented to humanity in religious ritual. Everywhere the mystery of metamorphosis, of transformation, meets most intimately the mystery of esoteric alchymy.

Here a pre-eminently important passage from the lectures-course *Anthroposophy, an Introduction* [Dornach. 19 Jan.–10 Feb. 1924. GA 234, Lecture 2, 20 Jan. 1924] touches on the central mystery of alchymy:

> You see, we may regard our physical organism as organized for taking in external substances—present-day substances—and excreting them again as such; *but it bears within it something that was present in the beginning of the Earth but which the Earth no longer has. This has disappeared from the Earth* leaving only the final products, *not the initial products.* Thus we bear

within us something to be sought for in very ancient times within the constitution of the Earth. It is that which we bear within us, and which the Earth as a whole does not possess, that raises us above physical, earthly life. It leads man to say: *I have preserved within me the beginning of the Earth.* By entering physical existence through birth, *I have ever within me something the Earth had millions of years ago, but has no longer.*

What Rudolf Steiner calls here '*Anfangsprodukte* — initial products' and '*Endprodukte* — final products' of the Earth lead to the *materia prima* and *materia ultima* of the alchymists. A most significant bridge to the mysteries is revealed at this point, a bridge that spans from the insights and teachings of ancient Indian yoga to that of the threefold human organism, as these lived with the Rosicrucian alchymists of the Middle Ages, and then again in a contemporary form in the anthroposophy of Rudolf Steiner.

The Rosicrucian alchemical teaching of the three principles or potencies *Sal, Mercur* and *Sulfur* — which are not simply the salt, quicksilver (mercury) and brimstone (sulphur) of the chemist — are reflected again and find their pre-eminent explanation in the anthroposophical teaching of the threefold human being:

- the system of the senses and the nerves (head),
- the rhythmic system (the breathing and the circulation of the blood), and
- the system of the digestion and the limbs (lower human being)

and their mutual interpenetration. This was first presented by Rudolf Steiner in the book *The Case for Anthroposophy* (*Von Seelenrätseln*. GA 21), written in 1917. The process of nourishment is intimately involved in all three systems, not only in the lower human being. All 'esoteric development' — as Rudolf Steiner shows and as was known already in Indian yoga — is connected with a refinement and spiritualizing of the process of nourishment.

Physical bodily nourishment with its mineral, its *salt* components nourishes the human being of nerves and the senses, the ego-point of the human head (*The Effect of Occult Development*. Lecture-course, The Hague, 20–29 March 1913. GA 145). In this lies one of the many sides of the Grail-mystery, which meaningfully connects with the mystery of astrology, the Christened wisdom of the stars renewed through Christ, and the mystery of alchemy, the wisdom of earthly matter renewed through Christ. A refined process of nourishment also lies in the 'rhythmic human being', in the *process of breathing*, which holds the middle between nourishment and perception, the function of the human being of nerves and the senses. For the Indian yogis all 'knowing the Divine' was still a breathing in the Divine, a breathing of the cosmic mysteries. How this refining and transforming of the breathing in the esoteric development of the 'working with the philosopher's stone' is related to the *mystery of carbon*, was touched on above. In Rosicrucian language,

- we are dealing here with *mercurial* processes;
- the lower human being of digestion has to do with *sulphur* processes;
- the human being of the nerves and the senses has to do with *salt* processes.

The physical component of salt taken upwards out of bodily nourishment is connected here (as explained in the lecture-cycle given in The Hague) with that which out of the refined processes of sense-perception as a spiritualized nourishment, is perceived *from above*. Christ's saying, 'I am the living bread of life that came down from heaven (*Uranós*)' (ἐγώ εἰμι ὁ ἄρτος ὁ ζῶν ὁ ἐκ τοῦ οὐρανοῦ καταβάς) acquires a perfectly understandable, thoroughly tangibly chemical, esoteric-scientific meaning. Also in the illumination of thinking in meditation there lay for the Rosicrucian a spiritualized salt-process. In his lectures on Christian Rosenkreutz (Neuchâtel, Sept. 1911. GA 130), Rudolf Steiner shows that purity of thinking, love, the meaning of sacrifice, are the spiritual counter-pictures of the formation of salt in the mercury-process (dissolution) and the sulphur-process (combustion). A bridge is indicated from the chymical to the chemical process:

- The mercurial element in the breathing, in the rhythmical human being, connects with a mystery of carbon dioxide,
- the sulphuric element in the processes of digestion, connects with the mysteries of nitrogen, thoroughly discussed with the farmers (*The Agriculture Course*. GA 327).
- There also connects with the process of salt (in the chymical sense), the esoteric principle of *sal*, a mystery of oxygen (touched on in Schmieder, *op. cit.* p. 7).

In this way, in the process of nourishment, when we correctly lay hold of it in its refinement and spiritualization over the whole threefold human being, the secret of alchemy lies hidden, unfolding itself as threefold, in the three potencies, principles, or processes of *sal*, *mercur*, and *sulfur*. In the midst of the 'dying Earth-existence' of the earthly world, showing in its condition today only the end products (*materia ultima*) of the earthly realm, of the 'dead Earth', the human being still carries in him/herself, mysteriously woven into the processes of life and nourishment, the 'living Earth' of the primal beginnings that contains the mystery of the 'initial product' of the *prima materia*, the 'virginal Earth', always sought by the alchymists in their ardent strivings.

To find practical access to these mysteries on the path of experimenting with matter was possible, as it seems, in earlier times. Then once again under special conditions of the time—whereby also star-aspects, everywhere so important for alchymy, play a role—it was possible in the Middle Ages in rare individual cases, in the face of numerous cases of cheating. It was possible when, with the outer experimenting, the outer transformation of matter and its purification, was connected to the inner transformation and purification of the soul, and at the same time with intimate knowledge of the aspects of the stars. There still existed a religious feeling towards the cosmic, as well as towards earthly matter; natural processes could still be experienced as a form of prayer. In our *contemporary* situation everything initially depends on finding the *point within* in a devoted spiritual work and meditation, which has always been mentioned in the present considerations with everything to do with the process of nourishment, with all processes with the threefold human being. Also to the farmers, Rudolf Steiner recommends a certain care of the meditative soul-life as a prerequisite for feeling into the intimate natural processes, as they are connected with the mysteries of nitrogen for the immediate practice of agriculture.

In [the activity of] thinking—this is the whole aim of these contemplations—we have initially today to find access to the mysteries, until a Christened natural science of the future will be able to bring forth these mysteries again. This will be the case when thinking [cognition], raised to Imagination and Inspiration is increasingly brought to the level of Intuition. A new Christened science of the stars will then be the decisive help for everything leading into the realm of earthly mysteries.

Today, words of primordial wisdom can also lead us on the way, such as the words of that mysterious tablet discovered in early post-Christian centuries that was dedicated by the alchemists to Hermes, the primal inspirer of the early Egyptian Mysteries, with its wisdom of the stars and of matter. It was called *Tabula Smaragdina Hermetis*. These words appear in *Die Geheime Figuren der Rosenkreutzer*, p. 17 [p. 244f.], as well as in the book by Schmieder. They are given in the Latin translation — which, if there is truth in the tradition, cannot be the original text — and on the basis of Schmieder's German rendering, read something like this [in the English tr.]:

> It is true, certain, and without falsehood; that whatever is below is like that which is above; and that which is above is like that which is below; to accomplish the one wonderful work. As all things are derived from the One Only Thing, by the will and by the word of the One Only One who created it in His Mind, so all things owe their existence to this Unity by the order of Nature, and can be improved by Adaption to that Mind. Its Father is the Sun; its Mother the Moon; the Wind carries it in its womb, and its nurse is the Earth. Its power is most perfect when it has again been changed into Earth. Separate the Earth from the Fire, the subtle from the gross, but carefully and with great judgement and skill. It ascends from earth to heaven, and descends gain, new born, to the earth, taking unto itself thereby the power of the Above and the Below. Thus the splendour of the whole world will be thine, and all darkness shall flee from thee. This is the strongest of all powers, the Force of all forces, for it overcometh all subtle things and can penetrate all that is solid. For thus was the world created, and rare combinations, and wonders of many kinds are wrought. Hence I am called HERMES TRISMEGISTUS, having mastered the three parts of the wisdom of the whole world. What I have to say about the masterpiece of the alchemical art, the Solar Work, is now ended.[31]

The maxims of knowledge contained in the old Hermetic wisdom saying 'as above, so below', and the *Tabula Smaragdina Hermetis* based on it, we find in a more tangible form in the 'golden chain of Hermes' (*Catena Aurea Hermetis*, presented pictorially, with pertinent remarks on the chemical material elements, with reference to details in *Die Geheimen Figuren der Rosenkreutzer*, p. 33 [p. 277f.]). In these pictures, the reader sees the whole grading of active cosmic forces from the divine-spiritual through the realms of the astral (planetary) and elemental (etheric) right down to the physical realm. This also helps us to understand why the 'philosopher's stone' is seen on the one hand as something completely supersensory and super-material, and on the other hand as something tangibly material. This *Catena Aurea* expressed how everything in the cosmos is connected and mutually woven together, as it were by an invisible golden chain [the 'great Chain of Being'], the smallest with the greatest, the most immediate with the furthest away, the finest with the densest, the most material with the most spiritual. In the 'gold' of this chain itself lies the mystery that connects the darkness of matter with the spiritual light — for gold is the direct revelation of the sunlight in the earthly-material realm. The 'chain' of the ascending and descending forces becomes for spiritual vision ultimately the great heavenly ladder on which the heavenly, cosmic beings in their heavenly degrees are revealed ascending and descending.

> To build the Whole how each part weaves,
> One in the other works and lives!
> How heavenly powers are rising and descending,
> The golden vessels to each other lending!
> Their pinions redolent with blessing,
> Down through the earth from heaven pressing,
> Harmonious all the All embracing![32]

Thus Goethe describes in *Faust*, Part 1 which is rich in alchemical motifs, the chymical mystery of the 'golden chain', of the *Catena Aurea Hermetis*.

How all these things lived with the early Mystery teachers and live again in anthroposophy, we can find, amongst numerous examples that could be listed, a passage from Rudolf Steiner's lecture, Dornach, 29 July 1923 [GA 291].[33] This helps us at the same time to understand the mystery of gold in alchemy in its cosmic depths and in its cosmic contexts.

> They (the early Mystery teachers) said: the human heart is a product of gold that lives everywhere in light; that which streams in from the universe actually forms the human heart. They imagined the light weaving through the universe carrying the gold. Everywhere in the light there is gold. Gold weaves and lives in light. When the human being stands in life … his heart is built up out of the gold of the light. And they [here Steiner concretely lists earthly substances of nourishment] are only the stimuli for the gold weaving in the light which builds up the heart out of the whole cosmos.

Nietzsche's deeply inspiring saying: 'The heart of the Earth is of gold'[34] also lies in the same direction as this insight in which the earthly mystery meets the mystery of the Sun, Moon and stars. Alchemy meets astrology.

How this meeting can be conceived, how in the light of Christ a new knowledge of the stars and of matter will one day be built up, we can see through the cosmogony of spiritual science, whose latent connection to the question of alchemy has already been indicated. Rudolf Steiner speaks in Neuchâtel, 28 September,1911 [GA 130] of the 'sacred natural science', of the alchemical Rosicrucians of the Middle Ages, of the authentic, genuine alchemists who experienced with their chymical experiments and processes a 'sacrificial mood, also great joy in the natural processes, also great sadness and released feelings', and how all this lies in the subconscious depths of our souls. If we follow the hints Steiner gave soon afterwards in the lecture-cycle *Inner Realities of Evolution* (Berlin, 31 Oct.–5 Dec. 1911. GA 132), then there lies in all the soul-drama and the scale of feelings experienced therein the soul-experience exactly referring to the range of the cosmogonic evolution of spiritual science: *Ancient Saturn, Ancient Sun, Ancient Moon*, and the *Earth*. Here lies the initiation experience that corresponds to the sum of what the pupil of initiation experienced in his own inner shocks and turmoil in beholding the cosmic processes of development, and at the same time inwardly participating with them in compassion.

With the continuing working in of the Christian impulse into the human soul there will come a time when what was experienced by the authentic adept in earlier centuries with the forming of matter during the chymical experimenting with matter as soul-tension and release will then be experienced *musically*. The as yet unimagined music of the future with its possibilities of expression will fashion the drama of matter, which for the initiate was at the same time a soul-drama. A new *music drama* of a Christian Mystery art of the future will be created. Indeed, in the lectures (*Art as Seen in the Light of Mystery Wisdom*. GA 275) Steiner says that 'in the final analysis genuine music is essentially a developing drama of life taking its course in musical sounds, which are an external picture of what the soul consciously experiences in the life of initiation'. In presenting this experience of initiation lies the actual task of the music of the future.[35] The human soul will one day 'be so involved in acquiring knowledge of the cosmos that it will experience shocks, losses and releases that will urge the soul to express in musical sounds that which can be experienced in portraying the path of initiation'. And we have heard how for the alchemical Rosicrucian the forming of matter was also connected with such experiences. A parallel exists between experiencing matter—cosmic experience and soul-experience—and musical experience and expression.

Thus alchymy as well as its exalted sister astrology would also have its musical side, when it speaks to us of its inner nature. Without our wanting to identify Wagner's music drama with the music drama still belonging to the future of the Christian Mysteries, we can nevertheless point out that with Wagner the initiation-experience (mostly the not-yet-completed initiation-experience ending in tragedy) seeks its musical expression more or less everywhere (already the ending of *The Flying Dutchman*, and most completely in *Tristan and Isolde*). In the *Ring of the Nibelung*, especially the alchymical side of initiation comes to strange expression. Already at the beginning of *The Rhinegold*, with the flashing up of the gold in the depths of the river, we are able to recognize this. Again especially at the end of *Twilight of the Gods* the stormy uproar of chaotic darkness can appear to us as the musical expression of chymical processes. Finally, after the regaining of the Ring through the Rhine-daughters, in the motif of redemptive love the pure flow of gold wrests itself free. This can be shown right into the key—the 'golden' D ♭-major at the end that connects with another loving D ♭-major carrying in itself the 'mystery of the gold of the chymical wedding' revealed in Act 2 of *Tristan and Isolde*.[36]

And we are reminded of Steiner's words, how the gold living in the light macrocosmically builds up the human heart, connects itself with experiences of love of the heart. This points to a spiritual aspect of alchymy that for an outer view easily loses itself in matter.

The whole context presented here between the chymical and the musical elements appears completely clear when we remind ourselves of the anthroposophical teaching of the etheric realm. The *chemical ether* (which in connection with the life-ether works as the chymical ether) is at the same time the *sound-ether*, the higher element of cosmic music. Schmieder's *Geschichte der Alchemie* mentions *Musique Chimique*, 'chemical music' by Flamel [c. 1330–1418].[37] The cosmic sound-forces we meet in spiritual science are, at the same time, the forces those in the first instance involved in the construction of the material world, the forces that order and group matter. To make this fact understandable, Steiner always pointed to the phenomena of the 'Chladni sound-figures' as physics explains it to us. Here this seemingly distant relationship has simply to do with facts.

III.

Alchymy and the Bible (Old Testament): The Creation, the River of Paradise, the Deluge; The secret of gold and of precious stones; Chaos and Astra, primal matter, the chymical process

The relationship mentioned above of the chymical facts and processes with those of the world-evolution and cosmogony, as it is made accessible to us today in Rudolf Steiner's *Esoteric/Occult Science* [GA 13] in a form corresponding to our consciousness today, also lived in the consciousness of the early alchymists. Steiner explains more clearly and in detail in the lecture-cycle *Genesis* (Munich, 17–26 August 1910. GA 122) the connection of this cosmogony in spiritual science with the cosmogony of the Bible, though, of course, drawing from a consciousness of another age. Accordingly, we should not be surprised that the alchymists of an earlier age in describing their chymical processes seek the support of the biblical cosmogony, and the Bible in general.

In alchymical and Rosicrucian writings of the early and later Middle Ages and the beginning of modern times, we meet this support everywhere, which can be perfectly understandable from the whole essence of alchymy. Amongst numerous examples, there may be noted *Die Geheimen Figuren der Rosenkreutzer* and Oetinger's treatise on the mysteries of salt.[38] An alchymical book from the eighteenth century, *Das gülden Vliess*, contains remarkable descriptions of the relationship of alchymy to the Bible.[39]

Its author calls himself *'Ichsagsnicht'* ['I do not say it']. (The exact title runs: 'The Golden Fleece, or the most sublime, most noble, art-enriched jewel and treasure of the wise of primal beginnings, in which there is shown for the discerning eye, and clearly presented, the general *materia prima*, and the same necessary preparation of it and the extremely rich fruit of the philosopher's stone, in a philosophical and theological manner described and summarized, through an unknown yet well-known *'Ich Sags Nicht'*. Nuremberg, Johann Adam Schmidt,[40] 1737.) The unknown author clearly relates how the chymical interpretation of the Bible was originally quite foreign to him, until the meeting of destiny with an expert in this realm, and the experience that arose out of this meeting taught him otherwise.

For the unknown author, it is not as if the Bible would *only* possess an alchymical meaning, but he now knows it *also* possesses it. And in truth, whoever seriously and without prejudice explores the realm in question and the writings — even though many things may appear as riddles or as problematic — will not be able to avoid noticing that the word of the Bible gains a depth of content from the concepts of these writings. Compared to this, the exclusively theological explanations of older and more recent times appear as relatively superficial ignorance. For the alchemical authors, the Bible becomes an exalted, coded writing containing the mysteries of the cosmos from the starry heights right into the depths of matter. These writings enable us to divine how in the Bible, besides the many other things it has to tell us, a *primal meaning of the stars* is connected with a *primal meaning of matter*. Between this stellar meaning and the material meaning there exists a most significant overarching relationship. In the present author's expositions on *Mark's Gospel* [MG] and *John's Gospel* [JG],[41] the attempt was made out of today's consciousness and thinking to lead the way again to this primal meaning of the stars and primal meaning of matter in the Bible, starting with the Gospels.

Alongside the New Testament, the Old Testament was of greatest significance for the alchymists, in the first place the creation story at the beginning of Genesis. Unlike any other biblical text, it places us before the mystery of the initial materiality, of the alchymical *prima materia*, where at the beginning *chaos* is said to exist, the as-yet-undifferentiated primal matter (*tohu va bohu*). How in this biblical description of chaos and of the divine primal procreation, primal star-meaning and prime material-meaning already meet, is raised into a clear light through anthroposophy.

In his *Agriculture Course* [GA 327] as well as the lecture-course on astronomy [*The Third scientific Lecture-course: Astronomy*. Stuttgart, 1–18 January 1921. GA 323] — both are mutually deeply connected — Rudolf Steiner speaks on the mystery of the fructification process with the human being and animal. He shows that in all seed-formation lies 'chaos'. In the protein of the egg-cell [*Geschlechtszelle*] the earthly matter has come, as it were, to a zero-point, and 'is brought into chaos'. We are reminded of the expression of the above-mentioned Rosicrucian writings, where 'nature has ceased'. The complication of the chymical formula of the protein bodies, which increases to a degree no longer rationally graspable, breaks up in itself, allowing us to recognize the same fact from the side of natural science. Rudolf Steiner, moreover, shows how matter — we note here the connection of this word with the cosmic *maternal* forces — at this point, where it has come into earthly chaos, again becomes receptive to the cosmic elements, the forces of the stars. All procreative and embryological processes consist of this raying-in of the starry forces; the chaos in the seed collaborates with the starry element of the cosmic periphery.

Astrology and *embryology* appear here like two mutually dependent poles of scientific observation that want to penetrate the mystery of life and how it arises (*Astronomy Course*). In the same sense, the juxtaposition of *chaos* with *astra* ('*Gestirne*' — stars) forms a fundamental motif of alchymical writings that we also meet in *Die Geheimen Figuren der Rosenkreutzer* [*op. cit.*] at every step. *There is a basic secret of alchymy at that point where the connections of the earthly material cease, 'enter into chaos', and where earthly being* (Wesen) *decays* (verwest), *into which the stellar context works.* Consequently, the meaning of the descending tendency in the chymical process, which brings the initial material into '*Fäulung*' or putrification, into decay, creates within the prerequisite for the other, ascending process of enlivening, the 'resurrection process' of matter. Rudolf Steiner always pointed out the purely linguistic depths in the word *verwesen* (literally 'un-being', decay). And so the simplest process of birth, or fructification, the becoming of chicks out of the egg and the secret of human birth, cannot be understood without the presence of the world of the stars and the influence of the forces of the stars. *Above the mystery of birth the star truly shines*, the star of birth, the star-mystery.

Just as human beings were on the point of forgetting this mystery of the stars, having already lost it in their conscious minds, it gave itself afresh to the earthly world out of heavenly heights in the birth at Bethlehem. In the Christmas and Grail lecture-cycle in Leipzig (*Christ and the Spiritual World and the Search for the Holy Grail*, 28 Dec. 1913–2 Jan. 1914. GA 149), Rudolf Steiner has impressively shown that astrology had there become possible again, become understandable again from a new and deeper vantage point. And when we take alchymy, as already at the beginning of the observations, a 'chymistry of the cosmic processes of birth', then its connection with astrology becomes ever more clear and evident. Only those initiated into a higher wisdom of the stars were able to become true adepts of the chymical art, where only the experienced laboratory experimenter, experienced in sensitive perceptions of the respective star-constellation and its changing influences was able to find his way through the many difficulties, hindrances and dangers of the chymical process. (See on this also the studies of Frau L. Kolisko, 'Das Silber und der Mond', contained in the bigger work *Sternenwirken in Erdenstoffen*).[42] The working of the stars into earthly substances — this was what such a chymical laboratory experimenter had to be able to observe, and this he could not do without a certain degree of clairvoyant perception. In the experimental research and work inspired by anthroposophical spiritual knowledge mentioned here, a path has been pursued which one day in the future, in a way which takes account of the scientific conscience of the time, can open to the seeking human spirit significant portions of regions that today are still covered by a veil.

We shall increasingly appreciate better how the beginning of the Bible already places before us this great motif of 'the working of the stars in earthly matter' (*chaos – astra*), and why the alchymists with the description of their processes sought models in the biblical account. A baptism text in Middle-Age Latin, published by Eliphas Lévi and also referred to by Rudolf Steiner, is on the whole informative for the question of alchymy. It brings to our attention especially clearly the relationship of the biblical and chymical manners of expression. It shows how all true rites and ceremonies are based on the chymical mysteries of the material world. The three chymical principles or potencies mentioned, of *mercury, salt* and *sulphur*, revealing the primal Trinitarian principle in matter, are reflected in the ritual trinity of water, salt and ash. This baptism text has already appeared in the present writer's *Der Ursprung im Lichte*, 1924 (Eng. tr. *Our Origin in the Light*, Temple Lodge, forthcoming):

> In yonder salt lies wisdom, and may it preserve our souls and our bodies from all decay, through the spirit of divine wisdom and in the power of divine wisdom; may all the created lies of the material realm yield before it, so that the salt of the earth and the salt's earth can become a heavenly salt... May the ash return to the source of living water to become fertile earth and let the Tree of Life grow, through three names [of heavenly splendour] *Nezah Hod Yesod*... In the salt of eternal wisdom, in the water of renewal and in the ash which lets the new Earth grow, may all things happen, through the Elohim, through *Gabriel, Raphael,* and *Uriel,*

throughout all cycles of time. May a transition space arise between the waters and divide the water from waters, above from below, and below from above, to work the miracles of the One. The Sun is its Father, and the Moon its Mother, and the wind carried it in its motherly womb. It rises from the Earth to Heaven, and returns from Heaven to the Earth. I implore you, Being of the Waters, to be a reflection of the Living God in His works, a source of life, and a washing-away of sins.

We notice especially the passage, 'May a transition space arise between the waters' (where some things are contained in the already-mentioned *Tabula Smaragdina Hermetis*) with reference to the biblical story of creation (Gen. 1:6). In his lecture-cycle *Genesis* (Munich, 17–26 August 1910. GA 122), Rudolf Steiner shows how in this 'division of above from below', this division of the elements of the sound-ether is at work, which at the same time is the chemical ether and, as we have seen in connection with the life-ether, the carrier of chymical activity.

The connection of the ritual trinity *water – salt – ash* with the chymical trinity, *mercury – salt – sulphur* is so to be understood, that:

- the *water*, as the principle of dissolution, corresponds to *mercury*,
- the *ash*, leading through combustion to renewal, corresponds to *sulphur*.

Above we discussed the arrangement of the three principles to the mystery of the threefold human being. This arrangement is reflected in the organism of the plant, insofar as the forces of the human head are revealed in the corresponding root-nature of *salt*, in the leaf-nature the mercurial quality, in the flower-nature the sulphuric quality. The heavenly trinity is revealed again in the earthly trinity and moreover, when we proceed from the threefold human organism,

- in the salt-principle (*sal*, root-forces, forces of the head) the Father,
- in the mercurial-rhythmic principle the Son, and
- in the sulphuric principle, governing the lower human being, the Spirit.

Angelus Silesius also refers to this:

Every plant reveals that God is threefold,
Here sulphur, salt and mercury in one we behold.
[C. W. Book 1, 257]

If we observe the connection of the 'ash' with the sulphuric element, which again exists in blossom and pollen, then Novalis' saying (*Frag-*

mente) receives a deep meaning: 'All ash is pollen; the [flower's] chalice is heaven.'[43] And such a word is lifted out of the sphere seemingly of feeling into the sphere of pure knowledge, the highest knowledge.

Furthermore, with the triune arrangement of the three chymical principles, the aspects cross over.

- *Water/mercury* corresponds to the Father-principle, in that it still contains the salt dissolved in itself. In occultism, Steiner once said, the cosmic sea can be represented as a 'drop of cosmic quicksilver' [*The Four Seasons and the Archangels*, GA 229, Lect. 2];
- *Sal* in Rosicrucianism is everything that is deposited out of solution, corresponding to the principle of the Son.

The salt-cube mystery of the spatial world in the revelation of Christ of the 'New Jerusalem' (Rev. 21) and its relationship to the 'philosopher's stone' was mentioned above. Into this plays the notion that the power of salt stems and overcomes decay, which has its spiritual counter-picture in the purifying power of pure sense-free thinking. We are reminded of Christ's words spoken to the disciples in the Gospel (Matt. 5:13): 'You are the salt of the earth.' In this way the mystery of the salt-cube, of the forces building up the future of the Earth, was connected for the alchymists with the mystery of Christ as the spiritual cornerstone. Matt. 5:14 also significantly mentions the 'city on the hill'. In a purely chymical context, too, the 'salts' appear to connect the metallic 'bases' with the non-metallic 'acids'. They are a kind of mediator, a balance between the polarity governing between the two kinds of connections with oxygen. In his book *Boten des Geistes*,[44] Emil Bock quotes Oetinger on salt, based on the saying of Christ, 'You are the salt of the earth':

> The tincture or the philosopher's stone is nothing other than a most sublime regained salt, which as earth has greater power than it would if it were thin as the magnetic air. The human being at the beginning was earth. Out of the dust of the earth, he is to become a re-born salt.

The triune arrangement of the three chymical principles *sulphur, mercury, salt*, appears directly related to the chymical process with Angelius Silesius in his verse:

> The Holy Spirit, he smelts; the Father, he consumes;
> The Son is the tincture who makes gold and transfigures.
> (C.W. Book 1, 246]

Here the Christ-Son principle is also related to the salt. In the creation story in the Bible the triune element is revealed from which we proceed for the chymical observations, as discussed in the author's, *Our Origin in the Light* (with reference to Dr Karl König, 'Versuch einer Darstellung der jüngsten menschlichen Embryonalentwicklung', *Gäa Sophia* 1927, p. 221).

*   *   *

From the first chapter of Genesis, from the chapter on the creation, we turn to the second, the Paradise chapter, where the description of Paradise is preceded by the narration of the second creation, the creation of the (at first only spiritually created) human being out of the element of earthly dust (*haphar min ha adamah*). This 'element of earthly dust' is interesting for the alchymists who relate it to their *prima materia*, the mysterious primal salt (or light-primal salt of Oetinger). The description of Paradise and the rivers of Paradise was already felt in earlier times to possess a deep chymical meaning. In Oetinger we find concerning this (*op. cit.* para. 34, in the chapter '*Von dem Strom in Eden*') the following:

> Oh delicious jewel! Oh splendid precious stone that can only be found in the River Pison … the precious gold with the two priceless precious stones … the true *sal metallorum*, the salt of nature, the salt of the wise, the science of the ancients … the gold of the gods, the gold of nature, the gold out of the country of the noble ones; moreover the salt meant here is something divine, a well of wisdom, a river of the sciences, and a spring of truth … It is the matter out of which God created Adam, the first human being … an *arcanum mysticum*, the noble life of the whole of nature and of all creatures, the quintessence of nature.

That one cannot take the biblical description of Paradise with its rivers simply as something earthly and geographical; that everything here still lies in the supersensory, in the border-realm of the physical and the etheric worlds — so important for alchymy — was already shown in the author's book *Our Origin in the Light*. What appears like an earthly, geographical description is only a picture for supersensory-physical and supersensory-etheric realities. As Paradise itself is the supersensory-physical existence, the fourfold stream of Paradise is none other than the primal ether-stream of the world that carries in itself the secret of the 'four etheric formative forces'. We know the relationship of these 'four kinds of ether' to the 'four elements' (of which we know that they are not the chemical elements). That is:

- the highest ether, the life-ether, corresponds to the lowest element — the firm earth, the 'element earth'. Likewise, in inverse relationship:

- the sound (chemical) ether corresponds to the water element;
- the light-ether to the element of air;
- the warmth-ether remains as the fiery element in the centre.

If we look from here to the 'four rivers, or streams, of Paradise', then the first of these streams as the upper ether, the life-ether, would at the same time have to carry in itself a relationship to the physical and carry the earthly secret in itself. In the biblical description this is indeed the case (Gen. 2:10–12 AV/KJV):

> And a river went out of Eden to water the garden; and from thence it was parted and became into four heads. The name of the first is Pison [Pishon. NIV]: that is it which compasses the whole land of Havilah, where there is gold: And the gold of that land is good: there is bdellium (*bedolah*) and the 'jewel [Heb.] *soham*'.
>
> ['The gold of that land is precious; gum resin and cornelians are also to be found there' (v. 12 NEB). '... aromatic resin (*or* pearls) and onyx are also there' (NIV).]

In the spiritual-etheric, primal realm of the earthly-physical, we find with *Pison* that stream pointing most to the physical of the four etheric streams of Paradise. We truly find the archetypal mysteries of the physical realm, the *mystery of gold and of the precious stone*. This river of Paradise can be little regarded as an earthly, geographical river, and this gold can be as little regarded as the usual earthly gold. The Bible says as much, that the case is different with this gold: 'And the gold of that land is good' (Germ. *köstlich*, 'precious') — we could also translate, '... is no normal gold'. Not normal, earthly gold is meant here, but the 'miracle of gold', the primal light-mystery of gold, that which lies between the etheric Sun-gold and physical earthly gold as the 'heart of the Earth'. The primal gold-mystery of alchymy is echoed significantly in the biblical description of Paradise. As the earthly stream is linked with the miracle of earthly gold — one recalls the gold in the sand of the Rhine — so is the etheric river of Paradise linked with the miracle of light of the primal gold, in the borderland between the physical and the etheric.[45]

Little as the gold of the Paradise river is only earthly, mineral gold, so little is the 'precious stone *soham*' only the usual 'onyx', which is the dictionary word. The *mystery of the precious stone*, connected here with the chymical mystery of gold, lies rather with the diamond, with the crystalized carbon (whose relationship to the 'philosopher's stone' was mentioned above). There is already the purely natural-scientific fact, that gold too, even if this seldom appears in this way[*], crystalizes in the octahedral-form of the diamond, pointing to such a relationship. Pure gold, from the planetary aspect related to the Sun, physically reveals a mystery of the purified inner soul, the 'pure gold-stream of the etheric-astral element'; the transparent carbon-crystal, the diamond — as each mineral crystal expresses the forces of the super-planetary 'crystal heaven' — reveals a mystery of the element of the spiritual ego in its immediate relationship to the physical human being. The diamond — meaning the dark coal transformed into the transparent diamond — speaks to us of the metamorphosis and elevation of the physical, organic realm through the strengthened higher 'I' or ego, of the *chymical mystery of Spirit-man*.

How this process of purification and metamorphosis at work in the physical, governed by the 'I', is also called the 'work with the philosopher's stone' (Rudolf Steiner) is related to the process of breathing and the mystery of breathing (Yoga), was developed above. From this it can be understood how the Indian word *ātman* (nom. *ātmā*), related to the German word *Atmen* ('breathing'), can mean the physical body and at the same *Spirit-man* (as the metamorphosis of the physical body worked on by the 'I').

- The primal investiture of the physical body during the Ancient Saturn evolution is connected with the mystery of hydrogen (H).
- The primal investiture of the etheric body, the primal etheric life during Ancient Sun evolution is connected with the mystery of oxygen (O);
- the astral body during the Ancient Moon is connected with nitrogen (N).
- In a similar way, the primal investiture of the 'I' occurred during the Earth evolution: in the fashioning of the living-organic element and that which is physically organic, the unfolding spiritual 'I' is connected with the mystery of carbon (C).

For this reason, in its description of the primal earthly existence, [called] Paradise, with the mystery of primal gold the Bible significantly weaves in the mystery of the primal precious stone. This is the mystery of the carbon diamond that lies between the spiritual realm of the 'I' and the physical realm. It may be recalled here that *Soham*, the name of that paradisal precious stone (the dictionary renders as 'onyx'), in another ancient sacred language of humanity, in Sanskrit,

---

[*] Because we more often meet smelted gold, *Tr. note.*

standing close to the original language, is called 'I am' (or, 'the one who I am'[*cf.* 'he who is'], *so' ham*).[46] The word also plays a role in Indian yoga, whose mysteries of breathing we have touched on, especially through the diamond. The reversal of the syllables results in the word *hamsa* 'swan', in Indian mysticism and in the mysticism of the Grail the name of the initiate, Spirit-man, the one who has realized the I-am in himself.[47]

In its description of the secrets of the paradisal river Pison, the carrier of the life-ether and the primal physical [forces], the Bible calls a third element between gold and the precious stone, the mysterious substance *bedolah*.[48] According to the dictionary this would simply be any kind of resin. The Bible also points out that little as the gold there is common earthly gold, and little as the precious stone *soham* there is a common onyx — also not the earthly diamond of today, but the super-physical, etheric primal carbon and primal diamond — as little can *bedolah-bdellium* refer to normal tree-resin, even if it were the most precious, noblest resin of all. Here the Bible itself gives us the key in which direction the [solution to the] mystery can be found.

The word *bedolah* occurs in two passages in the Bible. Besides the chapter on Paradise, there is only Num. 11:7. Here it is said of the mysterious heavenly feeding of the Hebrews wandering towards the Promised Land, of the *manna in the desert*, that it appeared '*as bdellium*' (*bedolah*). With this paradisal substance bdellium, we consequently find ourselves — the Bible itself tells us — in the immediate vicinity of the star-mystery of manna, about which more can be found in the author's JG, p. 144ff. The stellar meaning of the Hebrew word man ('manna') is also pointed out, and the star-root √*man* 'thinking' (in Indian, *manuṣya* 'human being'). In all these secrets of the biblical manna, of which the Bible itself tells us that it touches the secrets of the Paradisal bdellium, we hear the motif of the *activity of the stars in earthly matter*. In both situations we find ourselves in the borderland between the etheric and the physical realms.

With reference to the mysteries of the heavenly sign of the Virgin, in which the Star, the essence of the life-etheric, touches that of the earthly-physical realm (which is why the Virgin in particular is the sign of alchemy), we could also call the borderland referred to here the *realm of the Virgin*. Nothing other than what we called at the beginning of these observations, the 'virginal mystery of the world of matter' stands before us. The *virginal earth* of Angelus Silesius, the *philosopher's stone* — as far as we do not mean with this the tincture, but the point of departure for its re-acquisition—the mysterious *prima materia* of the alchymists, stands before us in that paradisal substance *bedolah-bdellium in the etheric primal picture. The biblical description of Paradise connects the mystery of the gold and the precious stone with the mystery of the philosopher's stone*, the *prima materia* sought by so many with ardent longing. It must still be possible today somehow to discover the paradisal primal realm, to be found spiritually. Those who find in themselves some connection with this lost world can find the way to this mystery.

All these details are not our concoction, but things about which agreement reigns in the writings of the alchymists and their biblical explanations (see '*Vom Strom in Eden*—The river of Eden', para. 34 in Oetinger, *op. cit.*). In the work of the unknown author of *Das Güldene Vließ* ('The Golden Fleece'), mentioned above, there is surprising confirmation of what was here independently found on 'bdellium' and its chymical significance. These verses relate to the *prima materia* of the philosopher's stone, which is identified with the biblical, paradisal 'bdellium'. It is worth noting how the same substance at the same time is simply called '*Thon*'.[49] This word, standing here in a specific chymical meaning with regard to the essence of the sound-ether, also called the chemical, or chymical ether, suggests a possible relationship of the word *Ton (Ton-Erde* = 'clay-earth') to the word *Ton* (= 'musical sound').[50]

> *Ein gemein Ding uns Gott geben tut,*
> *Welches ist der Natur höchstes Gut,*
> *Der Welt bisher blieben unerkannt,*
> *Die es doch täglich bei der Hand,*
> *Vor Augen allzeit an dem G'statt*
> *Allenthalben das Thon liegen hat;*
> ...
> *Sein Nam wird etwas genennet Thon,*
> In heiliger Schrift Bedellion.
> ...
> *Rührt her vom Mond- und Sonnenschein.*
> *An der Farb grün, grau, weiß und rot.*
> *Wenn du kennst solch edel Kleinod,*
> *Das ich genennet in der Summ,*
> *So hast du das recht Subjektum.*

∇

> *Dieses Steines Geschlecht ist allenthalben;*
> *Seine Empfängnis geschieht in der Höllen;*

Seine Geburt hat er auf Erden;
Sein Leben führt er im Himmel;
Sein Sterben erreicht er in der Zeit;
Nachdem erlangt er die Seligkeit.
Ich Sag nichts mehr.

* * *

[A common thing God gives us,
which is the highest possession of Nature,
by the world it was hitherto not recognized,
yet daily it lies to hand,
before our eyes in the action
always where *Thon* — clay, and/or musical sound — exists;
. . .
Its name is *Thon*,
in holy scripture bdellion.
. . .
It originates from the moonlight and sunlight.
In colour green, grey, white and red.
If you know such a noble jewel,
which I have summed up,
then you have the right subject.

∇

The species of this stone is everywhere;
its conception occurs in hell;
its birth takes place on Earth;
its life is led in heaven;
its dying it achieves in time;
after which it achieves blessedness.
I say no more.]

* * *

The description of Paradise in Genesis places before us primal chymical facts. The primal mystery of light of all earthly material, its 'origin in the light', helps us to divine the primal affinity of light especially to gold and coal (diamonds). The description of Paradise significantly places between the chymical mystery of gold and of the precious stone that of the 'virginal Earth', of the *philosopher's stone*.

The story of the 'Fall of Man' follows the story of Paradise. It results in that great crisis in the evolution of the Earth, which in esoteric tradition is called the catastrophe of Atlantis and in the Bible the Flood, or the *Deluge*. It lives on in the myths and myth-making memories of almost all the peoples on the surface of the Earth. As in the processes of the primal creation itself, the alchymists also find in these great crises of evolution and catastrophes of the Earth, creating a new configuration of earthly material and elements, an archetypal picture of all those crises of the material elements which they live through in carrying out the chymical process. Indeed, precisely here the relationship of the chymical to the cosmogonic realm appears especially clear in all its details.

Through the great catastrophe of the Flood a kind of renewal and rejuvenation of the earthly existence enters right into the material element. Atlantis that dissolves in chaos is renewed and rejuvenated in the youthful epoch of the first post-Atlantean age. In the manner in which esoteric research describes the foggy atmosphere of ancient Atlantis, where water was still lighter and more airy, where the air was more watery than today, many things remind us of the descriptions which the alchymists give of the chaos of matter of their initial substance (*prima materia*), whereby the predicate 'misty-watery' plays a main role. Out of the chaos of the catastrophe of the Flood, a new division of the waters, the airy element and the solid earth was fashioned. The alchymists also sought to lead their 'chaos of matter of the misty and the watery' towards a new division and grouping of the elements. They helped themselves in their technical descriptions of the process with a special preference for the picture of the story of Noah.

With this opportunity, let us keep in mind the 'chymical process', as it took place through the six or seven stages, of:

> *Mortificatio* (killing of matter),
> *Putrefactio* ('putrification', bringing matter into the forces of decay),
> *Solutio* ('dissolution'),
> *Animatio* ('re-enlivening'),
> *Purefactio* ('cleansing, purifying, elucidation'),
> *Perfectio* ('fulfilment'), and
> *Fixatio* ('attaching', fixing).

The last two processes are most likely taken as one. Like a scale of soul-experiences experienced within, which could seek expression in music, the chymical process is manifested outwardly in a scale of colour-experiences, in a characteristic changing play of the colours of matter. Matter was brought towards its 'dying', its decay; a black colour was formed, the 'head of the raven'. When finally, after the dissolution, re-enlivening and purification, out of the 'bridal bed of the chymical wedding' the miracle of the 'red lion', the 'kingly stone' of the red tincture, has arisen, a certain revelation of colour of white and red appeared. In his *Theory of Colours*, Goethe also refers to this: 'The highest white is transfigured in the red.' Before this, a *rainbow* appeared (also called the 'peacock's tail'), a miracle of colour traversing the whole scale of the rainbow, which after long and often dangerous experimenting gave hope to the laboratory experimenter for his final success.

Like the black head of the raven, compared with the raven of the story of Noah (Gen. 8:7), the chymical 'rainbow' is also connected to the story of Noah (Gen. 9:12ff.), which appeared as a phenomenon for the first time in the becoming of the Earth, in the new division of light, air and cloud, and which shone as a light-symbol for humanity's renewed hope for the future. Other pictures of the story of Noah also found a chymical interpretation, especially the *dove* (Gen. 8:8ff.) as the picture of the new life coming from above, from the forces of heaven . That which dies in Earth-existence is renewed out of the cosmos , corresponding to the dove in the Grail-Mysteries, according to the above-mentioned [Chapter 1] Grail-seal.[51] In Rudolf Steiner's explanations, the dove is the pure spiritual cosmic being for which the human being prepared himself as an earthly chalice or vessel.

As the most eminent amongst all the numerous presentations in the literature of alchymy, overreaching each other in riddling obscurity of the above-mentioned *chymical process*, the well-known 'Parabola' appears in *Die Geheimen Figuren der Rosenkreutzer* pp. 44–5 [p. 300ff.], selected there as the final quintessence, expressed in words, of this Rosicrucian wisdom. Purely pictorially, clothed in poetic Imaginations, the Parabola through its whole style right from the start makes it quite clear that it cannot, and may not, make revelations in the slightest [degree] to the intellect in sensory descriptions of outer events, but it only turns towards the Imaginative soul-capacities that are to be achieved on the path of meditative effort. A key to the cosmic riddle is only offered to the one who going through Imagination to Inspiration and Intuition makes towards the last-mentioned highest kind of knowledge.

Already the beginning of the Parabola makes the mystery pictorially clear to the one seeking the path of knowledge. On a rough footpath, he is driven forwards by a strong wind irresistibly, finding again on a lovely meadow (*pratum felicitatis*) the circle of the wise, who speak amongst themselves 'of a high and great secret hidden in Nature, which God conceals from the wider world, and only reveals to a few who love Him'. Here the seeker is first tested on his ability to think, then led before the *Lion*, whom he has to cut up and bring back to life again. Then a dangerous ridge-walk is mentioned, where many fall headlong. From details of the narration, it clearly emerges that the mystery of male and female plays a role, which in *Die Geheimen Figuren der Rosenkreutzer* appears right at the beginning as the first of the mystical pictures p. 3 [p. 216f.], in a clear connection with the question of the kinds of ether (the four coloured triangles). This is followed by a picture of red and white roses, which mostly grow in a garden enclosed behind a wall. Many people crowd before this wall, who have to carry out useless and dirty work — thus the seeker now knows, he also has until now done nothing other, nothing better in his life.

Only a small opening, not perceptible to common sight, offers a secret entrance with a skeleton-key prepared especially for this (is it the weapon of the 'I' in the mystery of Parsifal?). In the great garden there exists a small, square garden, where the roses blossom, above which spans a rainbow in the Sun-glittering play of the drops of water. The most beautiful maiden leads the most comely youth by the hand. The well-known motif of bridegroom and bride and of the chymical wedding forms the ending, which instead of a bridal bed is carried out in a transparent, clear crystal cell, which is like a heavenly sphere.

The lovers go through a mystery of death and resurrection, dissolving in love they move towards death. Before this, a *Water of Life* is mentioned that streams from a mill with ten water-wheels, and at the end quickens the King risen again in new splendour (for the alchymist this is the *King of the Red Tincture*, the *Red Lion* risen again). It is natural to think here of the esoteric soul-organ, the [chakra] of the 'ten-petalled lotus-flower' (also described by Rudolf Steiner in *Knowledge of the Higher Worlds: How is it Achieved?* [GA 10]), which the Indian calls *maṇipūra* ('crystal shaft' [or 'jewel-city']), that organ which is connected to hidden forces and characteristics of nature, that is, with the 'chymical' context. All these connections suggest Christ's saying: 'He who believes in me (sinks the security of his heart into the "I"), out of his heart shall flow rivers of living water' (John 7:38). Physiologically, this soul-organ is oriented towards the Virgin (solar plexus), that is, towards that [star-]sign which as the sign of the earthly mysteries is *the alchymical sign, the sign of the heavenly forces that are revealed on Earth.* (The planetary ruler of this sign [♍] is Mercury that likewise governs alchymy, co-governed by Saturn and Venus; the context here will become clearer in the next chapter.)

In this Parabola, apart from the rainbow there appear still other motifs from the story of Noah — from which we take our bearings — like the 40 days when 'the waters assuaged' (Gen. 8:6 AV/KJV). All the pictures are so given that the purely material meaning which they also contain (that is, the 'melting together' of the lovers points towards the heating procedure during the chymical process), cannot be found without another, a spiritual meaning, revealing itself along with it. This is a sign of the true Rosicrucian alchemy. The 'Parabola' belongs to its most significant documents. The crystal-cell of the lovers, which then becomes the crystal coffin and resurrection coffin, causes us to think of the 'crystal-bright philosopher's stone', reminding us of the 'glass coffin' (this is the crystal coffin) in the fairy-tale of 'Snow-white', where we also find again the chymical motifs of the raven and the little dove from the story of Noah. We suddenly recognize how our fairy-tales, too, are penetrated by chymical motifs, indeed, how some of them seem to be inspired directly from the alchymical-Rosicrucian side. This also applies to Goethe's 'Fairy-tale of the Green Snake and the Beautiful Lily', which shares many motifs with the Parabola of the Rosicrucians. As in the Parabola, the motif of the 'chymical wedding' can be found, especially in 'Snow-white' and many other fairy-tales, for example, in 'The Crystal Ball', where already the name contains the main chymical motif of the Parabola. And a highly interesting presentation of the chymical process appears in a somewhat shortened form in this fairy-tale — [also in] the story of the Firebird and the Golden Egg, and so on — so with 'The Crystal Ball' we have before us probably the most significant of the 'chymical fairy-tales'. The 'motif of the white and red roses' — the motif of the 'white and red tincture' hidden within — appears in the fairy-tale of 'Snow-white and Rose-red', which, regarding the chymical relationship in general is deeply significant. 'The Seven Ravens', too, are mentioned by the Rosicrucians themselves as a 'chymical motif'. This can all be rightly understood, and we shall not trespass upon the natural simplicity of our fairy-tales too closely, when we consider how especially in the chymical content the most spiritual content unites with the most natural.

* * *

The Bible, with the cosmogonic section at the beginning including the story of Noah, contains the actual main chymical motifs; the alchymists also find connecting points everywhere in the later sections. Only a few things may be mentioned here. A famous motif always taken by the alchymists for their *prima materia* are the words of Isaac's blessing, of the '*dew of heaven and the fatness [richness, NEB] of the earth*' (Gen. 27:28 AV), *cf. Die Geheimen Figuren der Rosenkreutzer*, p. 48 [308f.]:

> The dew of the heaven and the fat of the earth is our art-subjectum or Materia. Consequently it is neither mineral nor metal; the Pythagorean indicates to us that there are two mercurial substances of one root: Fire and water, Ischschamaim, namely [see Illust.], drawn out of Minera, wherein all metal and minerals are situated. It is a dew of heaven, but a mineral and metallic dew of heaven, in which are all the colours of the world, which may be coagulated through artificial operation into a sweet salt, called Manna, into a medicine; Sol pater, Luna Mater, from both these it receives its light, life and splendour, its fiery light-essence from the Sun, from the Luna its watery light-essence. We find it coagulated and dissolved. This dew falls from above into the depths of the earth and its body is made up from the most subtle parts of the earth. From above this dew receives its soul, and spirit, fire and light go into its salty body, receiving the powers of the things from above and below (nempe Virtutes Substantiales). To our eyes appears this mineral-dew in white, yellow, green, red and black colours, these being the only colours visible to our outer eyes. For it appears corporeally to the outer eyes, at times seen by miners in the mountains, appearing to the outer eye, heavy, watery, and dripping. Neither the miners nor artists know to what use to put it, since they do not know for what purpose Nature placed it there, nor of what sex it is, nor whether it be mineral or metal; all this is incomprehensible and unrecognizable. The best dew is that which in colour looks like coagulated electrum or transparent amber. What the world uses it for I do not know, yet it is with all its power in all things. The dew itself is always rejected and despised; it separates into two branches, white and red from a single-root, and stands upon this single root, growing like a white and red Rose of Jericho and blossoms like a lily in the valley of Josephat, oft-times broken off untimely by miners and is tortured by ignorant work-men. The true artist knows its influence, and plucks it in full bloom, with blossom, seed, root, stem and branches, namely: In full bloom, through the faith of the inner opened eyes. This is enough said of its bodily form: It is neither metal nor mineral, but nevertheless first mother and material of all metals and minerals.

Here, too, there is abundant reference to biblical passages and biblical language is noticeable in the details. In the Pentateuch, especially the story of the *burning and pulverising of the Golden Calf* (Ex. 32:20), which

the alchymists stubbornly laid claim to (reverse of the chymical process, *Aurum potabile,* and so on), on the grounds that Moses was indeed
a pupil and initiate of Egyptian wisdom and of the chymical art. Yet the
context here is not completely clear, and even Schmieder in his
Geschichte der Alchemie, p. 46, puts a question mark against this story.

More important from the chymical aspect is the story of the building
of Solomon's Temple and of the architect Hiram. In his mystery-drama
Hieram und Salomo [1st ed., Dornach 1925], Albert Steffen poetically
developed in particular the significant chymical motifs of the 'molten
sea' ['sea of cast metal', NIV] (I Kings 7:23ff.; 2 Chron. 4). A clear
chymical motif is contained in Oetinger's book on the mysteries of salt,
recalling the miraculous story of Elisha, 2 Kings 2:19–22 [healing of the
spring, involving salt]. The 'motif of the white and red roses', of the
'white and red tincture', the alchymists find especially in the flowery
language of the Song of Songs, completely taken up by them in a
chymical interpretation: 'I am the ['a', NIV] rose of Sharon, and the ['a',
NIV] lily of the valleys' (AV). This saying, together with the figure of
Christ and a red rose, is found on the title-page of *Die Geheimen Figuren
der Rosenkreutzer;* [relating to] *'mein Freund ist weiß und rot'* ('My beloved
is white and ruddy') (Song 5:10). And in the Book of Job and in the
Apocrypha the alchymists find many of their mysteries.

* * *

IV.

Alchymy and Mythology:
Isis; *The Rhinegold*; the Golden Fleece; Venus-Urania

Isis

The 'activity of the stars in earthly material', once the dream of the alchymists, was justified by individual 'workers in the vineyard' in humanity's evolution; they are still isolated today. By patient attempts they brought this work on to an experimental basis justified before the research methods of modern natural science. These individual workers were open for what was to come. The alchemists' dream lived pictorially in the past in myths and sagas as a great primal memory of humanity. Through ancient myths and mysteries, there runs something like a great astrological-alchymical, primal motif of humanity, a resounding of ancient, primal mysteries of the stars and primal mysteries of matter.

We speak today of the veil of *Isis*. For the consciousness of people today, the realm discussed here is deeply hidden by the veil of Isis, which at the same time is a *veil of the stars* and a *veil of matter*. Saying this, we have named the Mystery in the most worthy, the most important of all the early Mystery countries for us today, ancient Egypt. Its original name (*chemi, chemet*) was given to the whole realm of *alchymy*, and *chemistry* that historically derives from it. (From the Egyptian also comes the Greek *chemeia* 'chemistry', which is then related to the Greek *chymeia*, from *cheo* 'to pour', *chymos* 'juice, liquid', which with the Arabic article *al* becomes the word *alchymie*. The fundamental meaning of the Egyptian *chemi, chemet*, is: black, black earth.)

Star-mysteries and earth-mysteries were united in the sacred name Isis, who at the same time was the Queen of the Stars and the Mother of Matter. Today we find the relationship of Egypt to the chymical primal wisdom more in the Mysteries of this name 'Isis' than in the documents expressly handed down — with which the wisdom of Hermes, the 'hermetic' wisdom of the priests of the early Egyptians, was very reticent (one recalls the expression 'hermetic seal').

From our contemplations hitherto, we have met the life-ether, linked to the chemical ether, as the actual *chymical ether* and bearer of chymical activity. It manifests physically in the lowest element of earthly material, as if it were enchanted within it. And thus the chymical mystery of earthly matter was linked in the Egyptian Isis with the essence of the highest life-ether of the stars. It was mentioned in the previous section, how in the zodiac this relationship of the life-etheric to earthly material is expressed in the sign of the Virgin governed by the planet Hermes-Mercury. The Virgin is also the sign of alchymy itself, the sign of the Mystery of the Earth. Co-governors (rulers of the decans [the name given to the three equal subdivisions of the 30°]) of this sign in astrology are the obscure Saturn, the Lord of the earthly forces and earthly qualities, and the radiant Venus, the Governess of the stellar life-ether and of everything starry and flowery, of the '*Blu-men-Sterne*', 'the flower-stars' in the earthly realm.[*]

For this reason Venus is also the planetary revelation of Isis—the Egyptian Isis-Mystery culture took place during the time when the spring equinox of the Sun, the beginning of the light in the rhythm of the year, lay in the sign of the Bull ruled by Venus—whereas its still higher fixed-star revelation, as given in an earlier 'fixed-star wisdom', was beside the bright star Sirius (*Satit, Sothis*), the star of the Virgin *Spica* ('ear of wheat'). This reminds us of the mystery of the heavenly Virgin with the sheaf, working right into the Gospel, with the mystery of the seed and of the heavenly Feeding [of the Five Thousand] (see the author's *Mark's Gospel: the Cosmic Rhythm*, Anastasi, 2015; Temple Lodge, forthcoming). Consequently, the esoteric side of Isis-Venus—or Venus-Mercury (Isis-Hermes), for these two planets, for aeons close to the Sun, were originally one—play such an important, indeed decisive, role in alchemy. This works right into the realm of the chemical elements (quicksilver and certain copper compounds) and into the physiological realm (according to Rudolf Steiner's indications ☿ influences the 'movement of breathing', ♀ the movement of the glands). Here, however, the influence with Venus is not for instance in the sexual sphere—this is governed by the Moon. Originally Venus had nothing at all to do with the sexual sphere; her influence is to be thought of in

---

[*] *cf.* 'Three things remain from Paradise: stars, flowers, and children'—Dante Alighieri—*Tr. note.*

another sphere. These relationships are to be found expressed especially in the chymical term *hermaphrodite* (Hermes = Mercury, Aphrodite = Venus), by which the alchymists named the 'philosopher's stone'.

When the star-revelation of Isis had vanished from the Mystery-consciousness of humanity, it continued to live in the plant-etheric realm, in the elemental realm of the plants on the Earth.[52] We are reminded of the planetary relationship of Venus to the 'flower-stars', to everything blossoming and flowering on Earth.

This revelation disappears as well in the descent of humanity; the flower of Isis sinks into the grave of the physical, mineral reality of the Earth, which for later human consciousness and thinking remains initially as the only immediate revelation of the natural world. Yet it becomes clear how in this entire earthly veil of matter Isis, Queen of the Stars, is revealed, when we recall how Rudolf Steiner once spoke in the lecture-cycle *The Spiritual Beings in the Heavenly Bodies and in the Kingdoms of Nature* [Helsinki, 3–14 April 1912. GA 136], Lecture one, on the *mystery of the 'Weben und Wesen'* — '*the weaving and existing of matter*' that is revealed in *snow*. Like no other sign in the 'great coded language of Nature' (the expression derives from Novalis, *The Apprentices of Sais*), the *ice-crystal of the snowflake*, woven out of tiny six-pointed stars and similar figures, reveals how out of the primal essence of the light-crystal of the upper regions—an earlier esotericism still spoke of a 'crystal heaven'—the veil of earthly matter was originally woven.

In the ice-crystal of the snowflake, we see as it were the starry veil of Isis becoming the veil of matter. At no other point of the realm of natural revelation do we touch the Mystery of Isis of earthly matter, the 'virginal secret of the material world' so pictorially and directly. And we become aware how those primal crystalline light-forces still divined in the snow-crystal have also found their physical expression in the quartz crystal, in mineral crystals generally. We understand more clearly what was mentioned at the beginning of these contemplations concerning the cosmic crystal-forces and their connection with the forces of space and forces of light with the 'crystal-bright philosopher's stone' (which is 'everywhere and nowhere'). From anthroposophy we learn how in the forces in the upper star-region and upper planetary (beyond Saturn) star-regions and star-realms the primal power and primal pictures, the 'egos' of the mineral crystals can be encountered.

In the last lecture of the cycle *Between Death and Rebirth* [Berlin 5 Nov. 1912–1 April 1913. GA 141], Rudolf Steiner pointed out how, from these realms beyond Saturn (the Uranos, or 'crystal heaven' of the early Mysteries), the forces also derive which in the progress of earthly cultures build up something like a new [spiritual] earthly body which is then ensouled by the Sun-forces of the Christ. This also leads into profound chymical matters of the Earth and of resurrection. In the author's essay 'The name Isis'[53] all these connections of the stellar element and earthly element, of the veil of the stars and the veil of matter, are shown to be already contained in the name Isis itself, especially in its Egyptian form 'H-S-T, which with vowels becomes Ist, Iset or Isit. The mystery itself, the divine archetypal stillness ('h, Aleph, an aspirate still on the borders of what is audible) seems to speak to us out of the consonantal form of this name. It seems to express how the divine-supersensory realm, the upper, bright star-being ('H) is at it were enchanted into the rigid, stony, dying mineral element of earthly matter (S-T). It was also pointed out how we can follow these connections in the German word Eis [and the English 'ice'] right to the sounds of Isis, how they are revealed in the fairy-tale figure of the Ice-Maiden. Moreover, the word crystal telling of these cosmic contexts and mysteries carries in itself the Egyptian name Isis (Ist), and with this the name [or rather, the title] Christ, that contains in itself once again the Egyptian name of Isis; as though we should read from all this how the primal forces of the light and of the stars in the crystal, taken up into the 'I' become Christ-forces there, chymically building up the Christ-future of the Earth and of humanity. (Further, on the esoteric context of 'Christ' and 'crystal', see the author's JG) [Anastasi, 2015]. *The virginal mystery of the world of matter*, the Isis-Mystery, can be newly revealed in Christ. The Apocalypse of John calls this virginal mystery, the revelation of Isis and revelation of Christ, of the ego-rejuvenated Earth (the 'New Jerusalem'), the *Bride*.

All these primal mysteries of the crystal and of light, and the Mystery of the stars and earthly matter, of Isis-Venus become in the sphere of Christ the Mysteries of Mary. This is referred by Angelus Silesius in the verse:

> *Maria ist Kristall, ihr Sohn ist himmlisch Licht,*
> *Drum dringt er ganz durch sie, und öffnet sie doch nicht.*
> [Mary is pure crystal, her Son celestial light;
> Wholly penetrated by him, yet unimpaired she shines.]
> [C.W. Book 3, 242]

If we hear these words together with the Medieval hymn of Mary, the 'Star of the Sea' (*Ave Maris stella*; quoted in the author's JG, p. 68), then meaningful esoteric contexts of the Isis-Mystery of the stars and the Isis-Mystery of earthly matter within the realm of Christ are revealed: *Isis*, the star sunk into the grave of the earthly world, the *star of the depths* appears rejuvenated afresh in *Mary*, the *star of the sea*, as the picture of earthly matter, purified and raised in Christ.

*   *   *

The Rhinegold

From ancient Egypt with its myths and mysteries, and leaving Greece aside for the moment, we turn now to Teutonic prehistory. At that time the *star of the depths*, the primal mystery of gold and the primal mystery of the light sunk and extinguished in the picture of the depths of the river in *The Rheingold*, is expressed by Wagner's music drama. In this connection, we recall how the gold in the sand of the Rhine is expressed by chymical motifs in the music, mentioned above [Chapter 2]. These pictures, spiritually reaching from the earthly up to the etheric primal realm, can again call the Paradise stream before the soul.

The saga meaningfully narrates how the Rhinegold was stolen by Alberich, King of the black elves and Lord of Darkness, from the Rhine-daughters, the innocent children of the depths of the primal stream. The depths of the Rhine appear here as the picture of the etheric primal stream. The gold is smithied into the ring, the picture of the earthly ego-personality. The 'star of the depths' is extinguished there. From then on the mystery of the depths is covered in darkness: the pure gold-stream of the astral in the etheric is troubled and darkened through the lower 'I', which the tempter snatches towards himself. The tragedy of humanity lies in this, that forces and beings raise the human being prematurely towards his free 'I'-personality. The virginal mysteries of nature, which were still open to the innocence of those primal times, are now concealed from human view. The veil of Isis spreads over these mysteries. In his consciousness, human beings, raised too early into the starry heights of the 'I', sink with the natural part of their being all the more deeply into the darkness of matter. This extinguishes the consciousness of the other [of the starry heights]. Wagner's *Ring of the Nibelungs,* especially *Twilight of the gods,* helps us to feel this tragedy of mankind, how gracefully yet serious, how childlike yet mournful the song of the Rhine-daughters in Act III sounds in the charming key of nature, F-major:

The sun-goddess
sends her bright-shining beams;
night lies in the depths:
once it was light
when, safe and hallowed,
our father's gold still gleamed there.
Rhinegold,
radiant gold!
How brightly you used to shine,
you hallowed star of the deep!

'Night lies in the depths' — how these words place the whole picture of the present-day consciousness of the human being before us, who, standing at the abyss of being, before the veiled riddle of nature, looks into the darkness.

The Golden Fleece

Again we meet the same primal motif of humanity with another people of a distant past on the Mystery-coastlands of the Black Sea, the Argonauts, the Greek-Colchis saga of the 'Golden Fleece'. In this, too, as Steiner points out, one sees the 'pure gold stream of the astral realm'.[54] This does not exclude the fact, as everywhere in alchemy — and the 'Golden Fleece' is in the most eminent sense a chymical motif — that here too it links with the spiritual viewpoint of the chymical-material realm. All these pictures intend to tell us that only to the pure does the pure open up; only to the virginal-soul does virginal Nature unveil her secret; only those who can find or produce in their own nature the 'pure flow of gold' — only these people can find the 'philosopher's stone'. Angelus Silesius expresses as much:

> *Den halt ich im Tingiern für Meister und bewährt*
> *Der Gott zu Lieb sein Herz ins feinste Gold verkehrt.*
> [Him I hold the proven Master of tingeing
> who turns his heart into finest gold for love of God.]
> [C. W. Book 3, 120]

In his lectures on Christian Rosenkreutz [*Esoteric Christianity and the Mission of Christian Rosenkreutz*. Neuchâtel, 27–28 Sept., 1911. GA 130], Rudolf Steiner touches on the fact how, during the chymical process, with genuine researchers a metamorphosis of the aura takes place, perceptible to the clairvoyant. Previously the aura appeared mixed, then as a single colour, initially of copper, then silver and finally shining gold. (With this motif, we believe we recognize the four Kings in Goethe's 'Fairy-tale', in the mixed-metal [bronze], the silver and the golden kings.) In her publication *Das Silber und der Mond* (Stuttgart, 1929), Intro. p. 26f.,[55] Lilli Kolisko describes, with reference to the chymical literature, a vision of the alchymist Zosimos,[56] who sees a 'copper manikin' arise out of the flask, constructed as an altar. This figure, through metamorphosis becomes a 'silver manikin', and finally a golden man. Here too certain similar motifs reach us in German fairy-tales. The mystery of the 'Golden Fleece' is brought closer to us through all these pictures.

In his lectures, mentioned above, Steiner emphasizes that 'the false alchymist only wanted to form matter; for the genuine alchymist it depended on the experiences undergone when forming the material'.[57] Now, we do not intend to omit the material side by following the spiritual side of alchymy as expressed in [the search for] the 'Golden Fleece'. Yet it was precisely alchymy, as a 'primal chemistry of the living element' that set the forces of the life-ether into movement, unlike the 'dead chemistry' of merely outer experimenting today, something simply disconnected from the human being. Like the living forces of the etheric, those soul-forces of the astral realm (astral means 'starry') were intimately involved in these chymical processes, that 'activity of the stars in earthly material'.

The world of the true Rosicrucians was still a *sacred* experimenting; in a manner unimagined by today's natural scientist, the experimenter's bench became an altar. Novalis comes close to this in his feelings, when in his story *The Novices of Sais* [Ch. 2], completely penetrated by the chymical spirit, he complains how today:

> precisely the most sacrosanct, the most solemn, and the most enchanting phenomena of nature are in the hands of such insipid individuals as our analytical chemists are wont to be! They, who with brute force rouse nature's most creative faculties — something that should be a secret of vitality, a mystery of sublime humanity! — This is so shamelessly and mindlessly called forth by such rough spirits as will never understand the miracle enclosed within their flasks. Only poets should ever have dealings with fluidity, and be permitted to recount its history to the ardent ears of youth; *the laboratory would then be a temple*, and with new-born love mankind would reverence its flame and its fluctuations and sing their praises.

Only he who brings this devotion to the mysteries of Nature was worthy to come into contact with them. Only the inwardly pure, prepared through all sorts of tests, was permitted to stretch out his hand for the *Golden Fleece*. For neither as in the outer realm of matter, at least as it is apparently the case, does a separation take place in the chymical realm from the world of the living, nor indeed, from the moral world. This is the great motif of humanity, sounding to us down the ages so significantly from the saga of the search for the Golden Fleece, from Greece to Colchis.

According to the saga, this Golden Fleece is guarded by the terrible power of a dragon. From one viewpoint, a subjective one, it is the powers of sensuality, greed and fear in the soul that the individual, who intends to approach the mystery, has to overcome. In objective spiritual reality we stand here before a transition realm, whose threshold is strictly and earnestly protected by higher beings who demand reverence. Every step that does not take place out of a conviction that can arise before these exalted guardians of the threshold, leads the soul to abysses that surpass everything in catastrophic frightfulness, that otherwise appears as the grievous element in human life.

In esoteric literature, this serious theme is repeatedly taken up in poetic form and in novels. The saga of the 'Golden Fleece' is so to speak the earliest 'esoteric novel' of this type, the earliest alchymical novel in world-literature. The alchymists have always clearly and consciously viewed and valued it as the chymical document. In these contemplations we have already met the name 'the Golden Fleece' as the title of an alchymical text, and it seems we shall still frequently meet it. Also the earlier mentioned 'Parabola' of the Rosicrucians refers to the saga of the Argonauts and values it as an alchymical document. In one passage it recommends the seeker of the chymical mystery to think of *Medea*, the magical adept of the mysteries of the Golden Fleece of Colchis, and how she 'would have made the dead body of Aeson alive again' [p. 45/302]. The seeker thinks to himself, 'If Medea is able to do such a thing, why should it not work with me?' Of course, here in the 'Parabola', all this is initially related to the chymical forming of matter.

The legend of the Golden Fleece is the main example of the alchymist's novel of earlier times. This type of esoteric novel in recent times is found today in those of Edward Bulwer-Lytton: *Zanoni* and *A Strange Story*.[58] Not the transformation of metals, but the life-extending elixir plays a main role here; this is indeed the other side of the 'great

Magisterium' of the alchymists. The 'secrets of the gold', too, are mentioned at times in the second of these novels. In both of them the tragic destiny is strongly described of the one approaching the chymical realm without a true calling and the required moral prerequisites. The same is the case of the recent novel by Gustav Meyrink, *Der Engel vom westlichen Fenster* [The Angel of the West Window].[59] The part of the story dealing with the past, which embraces the *two* earthly lives of the main characters (the other part plays in the present day), takes us to the time of the Emperor Rudolf II [of Austria], the alchymist. It presents the deepest abysses of the alchymist's destiny. John Dee and his helper Edward Kelley, who, as uninitiated, possessed the tincture but not its secret, are both historical personalities (further details about them, Schmieder, *Geschichte der Alchemie. Op. cit.* p. 302ff.).

In the novel, the way the personality of Emperor Rudolf is described and his relationship to the alchymical strivings of the time shortly before the Thirty Years War, is remarkable. With Meyrink the illusionary 'angel from the western window' itself is the power that threatens and poisons the human soul — still in the present day, indeed to an increasing degree. It works against the impulse of the 'I' by spreading a fog over the consciousness in the soul, wanting to give it over to the opacity of magical enchantment. Not in the obscured ways of this daemonic-illusionary 'angel' — who is the unpenetrated part of our own lower being — but only with the full conscious powers of the awake 'I' (the pictures of the Rosicrucian Parabola speak of this, too) is it possible to approach the chymical secrets in a healthy manner. In the Greek saga of the Golden Fleece we already meet a decisive motif: the fleece and the secret of the treasure of gold, gained not through one's own power (the strength of the 'I') but through a strange magic in the dampening of the forces of consciousness, for the 'fortunate recipient' actually brings misfortune upon misfortune; destinies are destroyed through it.

* * *

Venus-Urania

On the ground of Ancient Greece, to which we were brought by the legend of the Argonauts, even if reaching into another distant mystery-realm, we find the *myth of Uranos* as a central mystery picture and picture of humanity in surpassing grandeur. It connects astrology and alchemy—the heights of the star-secret and the depths of the secret of the Earth. This myth, on the one hand has taken into itself the quintessence of the Egyptian Mysteries of Isis and its esoteric side. On the other hand, already like an entrance to Christian esotericism and the cosmic revelation of Christianity, it has taken into itself the presentation of the cosmic rhythm, of the star-mystery and earth-mystery in John's Gospel. By so doing it can be located as the central motif. Of course, according to the viewpoint from which we proceed, such a myth contains everything and nothing. Only patient and devoted meditative work opens up the depths of its content, the richness of its mysteries, the abundance of its contexts. It is with this [myth], as with astrology and alchymy in general, which can essentially never be turned into bookish knowledge (which is why all the literature on this subject is questionable and critical), but only into intuitive insight, that gradually opens up to devoted, esoteric-meditative work, where the right conditions of destiny are given.

The myth, summarized in the author's book on John's Gospel (JG, p. 46, p. 67), runs as follows: Uranos (heaven) is the father of Saturn-Cronos, who is the father of Jupiter-Zeus, the ruler of the gods and of human beings. Uranos is violated by Saturn-Cronos and castrated. Out of the starry-semen of Uranus that had fallen into the sea to become the froth of the sea, Venus-Aphrodite was born, Venus-Urania. [The study on John's Gospel continues:] We distinguish Uranós in the spiritual sense, the spiritual Uranus-sphere, as the sphere of the upper heavens beyond Saturn, from the mere 'Uranus planet'.

We recall how in Greek Κρόνος, Kronos [the Greek chronos also means time], the cosmogonic characteristic incorporated in the Greek myth of the violation of Uranos through Saturn-Kronos, coincides with the cosmic primal division, the cosmic primal Fall (though here, basically a language doesn't exist that could describe such an event) when Ancient Saturn-evolution becomes time, as spiritual science teaches. The original Saturn is still completely without time, is still in the Eternal, with the Father, is still united with Uranos (from whom the planet Uranus, that later came to the solar system, received its name). In the starry realms of Uranos, with the creator Beings of the world, whose original sacrifice at the primal, very beginning of the world, in the primal fire of Saturn-existence there is also the source, the true primal homeland of human beings. Only in the acquiring of time of [Ancient] Saturn, in the fall into time, does it take in the first foundations of the later earthly becoming—then still aeons distant.

As the starry and heavenly element is divided from the earthly and temporal element, from now on *Uranos* and Saturn are divided. The planet Uranus stands today as it were as the cosmic boundary-marker to the realms beyond Saturn in the supersensory realms. These 'realms' can no longer be conceived as earthly-spatial, divided from Saturn from whom today all influence of the earthly element and the weight of the Earth proceed. The relationship of Saturn to lead (as well as gold to the Sun, silver to the Moon, and so on), always assumed in alchymy, is today taken on to an exact experimental and scientific basis by L. Kolisko. Many reasons confirm that to Uranus we may ascribe radium that is gained from uranium ore; the element of 'emanation' and 'higher radiation' in general is important for all alchymy of the future. Consequently, the name chosen for the element uranium would have been no mere coincidence.[60]

Saturn, the representative today of 'Ancient Saturn', as presented in *Esoteric/Occult Science*, was the original Earth that included the whole solar system in its becoming. Cosmically seen, it is also today still simply 'Earth', indeed, it is the strongest expression of the earthly element in the cosmos. And only on the other side of Saturn could one search for what in the cosmic sense is super-earthly, that which is heavenly (for this reason perhaps what is on the Earth, in the earthly material world, is reflected in the 'supersensory'; one thinks of radium, electricity, and so on). And so all the planets of the 'planetary septenary' (bounded by Saturn) — viewed astronomically, we can only speak of an 'awareness of five' [Saturn, Jupiter, Mars, Mercury and Venus] — are basically still earthly, siblings of *one* cosmogonic primal family, leading back to Ancient Saturn, as the original, primal Earth.

This also corresponds to an unbiased outer view, that the starry nature of the actual heaven of stars (Uranos), the fixed-star heaven, is not to be found in the planets: the pale Saturn, the sombre red Mars, the sun-like Jupiter — to intimate observation, none have any actual 'star-nature'. Yet if a planet does reveal this starry element towards the Earth, then it is Venus, our friendly morning and evening star. Already the Indians, especially Buddha, recognized in her this stellar, super-earthly quality. Thus the outer heavenly picture prompts us to surmise something of the depths of the Greek Uranos-myth.

It is also significant for the deeper understanding of alchymy that we are able to experience in the feelings, especially *religiously*, the great cosmogonic and human pictures of the Greek myth. The picture speaks to our deeper heart-forces — which are the 'forces of gold' within us. It wants to tell us something concerning the great separation of the 'lost son', of the human being, concerning his Fall into the earthly element, his long and destiny-laden, dark and sorrowful wandering through the realms of the ages — realms of Ancient Saturn, Ancient Sun, Ancient Moon and the Earth as the stages of evolution of the Earth, separated by aeons, as described in *Esoteric/ Occult Science*. Eternal love, the love of the Father, of Uranos, did not want to leave the 'lost son' alone without the comfort of heaven after the separation. For this reason the Father shared the spark of heavenly fire of Uranos, *love* in the dark earthly realm, as a gift of light and gift of the stars. Out of the starry semen of Uranos fallen into the cosmic ocean, arises Venus-Aphrodite, the one born of the foam of the waves, the star of the sea, *Venus Urania*. The divine primal mystery of love is hidden in the Uranos-myth.

Does not this primal secret of love live especially in the picture of *Father*, *Mother* and *Son*? This well-known picture is at the same time the esoteric expression of the mystery of the Trinity, that in its usual, exoteric version as 'Father, Son and Holy Spirit' is frequently so difficult for us to understand. Here:

- the 'Father' is the will-empowered, masculine, creative side of the divine;
- the 'Mother' is the 'Holy Spirit', as the cosmic-virginal, divine womb, the feminine principle.
- The 'Son' is not, as the word leads us to suppose, only simply the masculine principle. As Genesis 1:27 describes, the 'Son' is the spiritual human being of the primal beginning, the offspring of divine creating (the 'Son of the Godhead — the image of God'): male-female, or to use the language of the alchymists: *hermaphrodite*.

On this point the whole picture of the Greek myth also contains depths of star-wisdom. For this divine primal mystery of the Trinity, of the Father, the Mother (of the 'Holy Spirit'), and the Son (of the 'hermaphrodite'), as it lived and lives beyond the threshold of Saturn and beyond time in the divine, primal being of Uranos, is revealed on this side of the threshold of Saturn, in the earthly-temporal and planetary aspect in the trinity *Sun*, *Moon*, and *Venus-Mercury*.

Here we think of the cosmogonic contexts of *Esoteric/Occult Science* and of the original unity of Venus and Mercury, of the two planets that for the longest ages have been connected with the Sun.[61] From earlier examples, we recall how alchymical writings mention the 'herma-phrodite' (Hermes-Aphrodite = Mercury-Venus), the 'philosopher's stone' whose 'Father is the Sun and the Moon its Mother'.

The original unity of Venus and Mercury corresponds to the con-dition of the human being *before* the (earthly) Fall of Man, the condition of the 'hermaphrodite'. The separation of the two would then corre-spond in the cosmic, planetary aspect to the human 'Fall of Man'. This goes back to the temptation by the (already fallen) Lucifer, or the Fall of Lucifer itself (that had taken place before the Fall of man). Venus, the heavenly (Uranian) jewel, falls out of the crown during the fall of the Lord of Light (who, during Ancient Sun evolution was still in the divine sphere, a brother of Christ). She reaches the vicinity of the Earth and at the same time the vicinity of Mars.[62]

Venus reaching the vicinity of Mars is the cosmic, planetary expression of what in human nature takes effect as the Fall of Man. From this all earthly longing arises, which has its cosmic origin in the longing of the Lord of Light for his lost star. Her strongly radiating beauty comes at appropriate times through her nearness to the Earth, brought into effect by this Fall, through the separation of Venus from the Mercury-sphere.

Between Mercury in the Virgin ♍ and Mars in the Scorpion ♏, Venus now stands in the Scales ♎ where her actual being is not reached by the daemonic Mars-powers in the sphere of the Scorpion. (The mythical entanglement of Mars and Venus, described by Homer [*Odyssey*, VIII 266–369], is an effect of the Fall only in the human being.) Everything of the lower sexual level, as mentioned before, has to do with Mars in the Scorpion, not with Venus. Also ♀ in the ♉ is some-thing different; it is the earthly revelation of Venus as the 'love in the primal beginning' and 'healing power of love' (as in the healing words of Christ in the Gospel; see the author's books on Mark and John). But in the Scales she is the heavenly, redeeming love, leading back to the original source of being, Venus Urania. This revelation of Venus most directly makes visible its connection with Uranos, according to the Greek legend. Here we stand again before the picture of the Venus-Aphrodite, born of froth of the waves, risen out of the billows, walking on the blue waves of the sea, in her maritime revelation as *Venus Urania*. We recall this connection of the Scales ♎ with the billowing sea appears everywhere in the Gospel. And we sense in looking at the picture of Christ in the Gospel walking on the waves, also standing in the Scales (Mark 6 and John 6), the whole relationship of *Venus Urania* to Isis-Maria as the portal opening from the Greek Uranos-myth towards the Christian Mystery.

All these astrological contexts at the same time touch on those of alchymy, about which we know that it is inwardly connected with astrology. We can also recognize in this the chymical meaning of the pictures to be seen in the Greek Uranos-myth. In these pictures we also find Venus-Aphrodite reflected in her original etheric purity *before* the Fall of Man, as the one rising out of the pure, salty element of the blue waves of the sea (which are a picture of the etheric-ocean). Here we recall how for Rosicrucian alchymy *salt* is a picture for the *purity of thinking*. And here we also find it in its original connection with Hermes-Mercury. Recalling the earlier contemplation [Chapter 2 above], in occultism the cosmic ocean carrying the bitterness of salt is the cosmic drop of *Mercury*. We find in this connection of Venus-Aphrodite with Hermes-Mercury the 'hermaphrodite', who, as we already know, the alchemists thought to be the 'philosopher's stone'. This bitter quality of salt speaks of a mystery of virginal purity, which we discover again in language in the name Mary (related to Latin *mare, amarus* 'bitter') and in its Hebrew form *Mariam, Miryam*, Miriam). Finally, when we think as well how in Venus-Aphrodite herself the flowering, blossoming element, the element of the pollen and with this the *sulphurous* element (as understood by alchymy) is also revealed, then we would recognize how in the picture of the Greek myth of Uranos, besides whatever else it has to say to us, also the alchymical trinity, *Mercury, Sal* (salt), *Sulphur* is expressed, which itself again expresses the divine Trinity in the world of matter. The Greek Uranos myth reveals — or hides — a Mystery of the Trinity. All this is related by the alchymists quite tangibly to the chymical mysteries of the respective metals ($\male$ $\female$ and so on); the connections of metals and metallic salts cannot be followed up here.

We feel the sublimity but also the dark side of all these pictures. The 'great secret', it seems, is revealed to everyone, and yet it remains, as Novalis says (in Klingsor's fairy-tale in *Heinrich von Ofterdingen*), 'forever unfathomable'. The tremendous picture of humanity in the Uranos-myth seems to give us a key to all the riddles of the world, and yet only the 'I' that is awakened in itself, strengthened and proven itself through the trials — we recall the Rosicrucian 'Parabola' — is able to unlock these riddles of the world. This indeed, as we saw, is the actual Mystery, the esoteric aspect of astrology as well as alchymy, that one cannot make book-knowledge out of them, but that they place us before this testing of the 'I'.

Venus, the actual being and carrier of all esoteric secrets, has moved out of its unity with Mercury into the vicinity of Mars. In the human being at least, she is entangled with the being of Mars, with the daemonic power of Mars, and only when the battle with these powers within the inner being of man can be won can we trace these mysteries. The story of an alchymical adept exists who allowed himself to be beheaded by someone who demanded the secret from him. He made this beheading the condition for his telling. In the [decapitated] head, between the teeth, a note was found: 'You can kill me, but cannot force my secret from me.' These powers of Mars that have to be fought in our own inner being are also the powers of death (*Mars* is related to [Lat.] *mors*, death). They are the dragon-seeds of the men in armour rising from the Earth with whom Jason, who desired the golden fleece, had to fight in the Argonaut legend, after he had overcome the fire-breathing bull. (Dragon and bull are the two adversary powers that also appear in other Mysteries). Wise and loving powers have placed these powers of death to serve the testing of the 'I' before the threshold of the Mysteries.

In all this lies the deeper reason why, as for millennia, even today the veil is spread over the Mysteries, especially of the chymical mysteries of the material world, why only few chosen ones in the past raised this veil, and why for the consciousness of people today alchymy has become something ungraspable and opaque, dismissed into the realm of superstition. And it would only lead to disaster, if it were possible, suddenly to reveal the mystery of human nature as it has become through its Fall, to give it into the hands of economic self-interest, of firms and 'concerns' ...

For this reason, the way to the Mysteries, still today as for centuries, is an esoteric one, to be struggled through within, consisting in embracing Venus, the bearer and protector of all esoteric work, released in one's own inner life from the restraints of the Martian powers and the powers of death, uniting again with Hermes-Mercury, the Lord of Initiation (as presented pictorially in the Greek myth). Then the 'hermaphrodite', the 'philosopher's stone' will be found. The revelation of the mystery of love, *Venus-Urania*, eternally unfathomable, was sought by the genuine alchymists right within the contexts of the material world (chymical wedding). It is linked and woven in the subterranean depths of the 'being of the spirit-ocean' (R. Steiner) with the mystery of death. It lights up when one passes through the portal of death — also to be passed through in the experience of the esoteric path. In the midst of the darkness and the ocean-storms of the earthly realm, it lights up as the star which is hidden in Uranos, the mystery of the lost origin of humanity in the stars.

And so in the Greek myth of Uranos the *meaning of the stars* unites with the *meaning of matter*. The virginal mystery of the world of the stars, Isis-Venus, is at the same time the virginal mystery of the material world, the 'star of the depths' sunk into the darkness of matter, veiled from the consciousness of humanity today: *'Night lies in the depths.'* In looking towards 'Maria, the star of the sea' and the picture in the Gospel of Christ walking over the waves we have already hinted in the direction in which the 'light that shines in the darkness' [John 1:5] is revealed. That light, in which also the 'mystery of the material world' can be revealed to us as a Christ-Mystery in the future of humanity, is the Mystery of the 'I', the human ego.

V.

Alchymy and the Future of Humanity: John's Gospel and the Apocalypse of John; The Mystery of Cana (Chymical Wedding) and the New Testament; The Mystery of the twelve precious stones.

Isis-Venus, whose star-mystery and mystery of matter is embedded in the Greek myth of Uranos, governs in the *Scales*, which in the Gospel (Mark 6 and John 6) is the sign of the waves of the sea. There she is the heavenly redeeming *Venus-Urania*, who bears the gift of the star-light of Uranos, the love that leads back to the primal source of all things. As such, she led us to the 'I-am' of Christ, walking on the waves. From this embracing picture of humanity of the Greek myth, she opens a door into the Christian Mystery, into the Christ-future of humanity. Suddenly we are standing in the middle of John's Gospel, the decisive document of humanity's future. For in truth the Scales, in which also the Christ's 'I-am' stands, is the rhythmical middle-point and fulcrum of this Gospel, as the author's book on John's Gospel shows. From the sign of the beginning, of the word in the primal beginning, Venus, who leads into existence, who is love in the primal beginning (♀ in the ♉) and the healing love in the words of Christ, has led the [cosmic] rhythm of John's Gospel down through the lower, darker signs following the Scales. There Venus is the redeeming Urania, who points again upwards, in order to return from below upwards to the beginning point. Thus the star that with Mercury is also the star of the chymical mystery, shines over the whole of John's Gospel.

One cannot present the [cosmic] rhythm of this Gospel without experiencing therein how the Johannine way unites star-mystery and earth-mystery. From the starry heights it leads down to the earthly depths, until over the earthly depths it begins again to light up the star-mystery. Thus John's Gospel, as the actual star-gospel, is at the same time the 'chymical' gospel. Not without deep meaning, where it initially suggests mythology, have the alchymists taken the writer of this

Gospel to themselves, calling him 'John the alchymist' (a name, which even in later times various alchymists have taken). And even the name Longinus, who in fact points to the central chymical mystery of John's Gospel—supposedly the name of the Roman legionary soldier who thrust the spear into the side of the Crucified—appears amongst the alchymists.[63]

In both chapters, one on the *Marriage at Cana* (John 2) and the other on Golgotha (John 19) containing the *mystery of the wound in the side*, the decisive *chymical motif of John's Gospel* appears, pointing towards the future of humanity. Like a red thread this chymical motif runs from the Wedding in Cana to the Cross on Golgotha. At the Wedding, the Christ-force metamorphoses 'water into wine', uniting with the Mother (John 2:3–5), the virgin maternal forces of the Earth, the 'virginal mystery of the material world'. At Golgotha, the lance of Longinus pierces the side of the Crucified, from which wound blood and water flows (John 19:34, 35, in addition 1 John 5:5–8). This chymical motif is already heard in the Old-Testament story of Moses, with the 'meta-morphosis of water into blood' (Exodus 7 and Rev. 8:8).

One can certainly keep in mind the spiritual side of this picture and be able to see in the water a picture of the 'primal waters', of the waters of the primal beginnings in the etheric, in the blood as well as in the wine, of the 'Sun-blood of the bunch of grapes': a picture of the personal ego-penetrated vision. In the author's presentation of John's Gospel, this more spiritual viewpoint (only one part of the chymical mystery) was emphasized. Yet the spiritual 'I'-processes—and this is the other, important side of the chymical viewpoint—have their counter-picture and counter-effect in matter. *The Christ-alchymy of the future is the alchymy of the 'I'*.

To explain the miracle of the Marriage at Cana, which he addressed from various, mainly spiritual, viewpoints, Rudolf Steiner once added that Christ's deed at Cana depended on the fact that the water used came fresh from natural sources that had not lost the elemental connection to nature (*The Gospel of St John*. Kassel 1909, GA 112, Lecture 9; see also the author's JG, p. 204 FN). Steiner says, 'A water that had just been freshly drawn had to be taken because, indeed, Christ is the being Who had just approached the Earth; He had just become acquainted with the forces that work in the Earth itself.' The Isis-seed, or sprout of earthly matter, unites with Christ's ego-power of the Sun. Here the *virginal mystery of Nature*, the mystery of the alchymical *prima materia* and its spiritual-physical transitions, is touched on lightly. This is a

Die Geheimen Figuren der Rosenkreutzer *(p. 3), involving the mystery of male and female, connected with the question of the kinds of ether (the four coloured triangles). See p. 51.*

TABULA SMARAGDINA HERMETIS.

VERBA SECRETORUM HERMETIS.

rhaftig ohne Lügen gewiß, und auf das allerwahrhaftigste, dies, so Unten, ist gleich dem Obern, und dies, so Obe
dem Untern, damit man kann erlangen und verrichten Wunderdinge eines einigen Dinges.   Und gleich wie alle
nem Dinge-alleine geschaffen, durch den Willen und Gebot eines Einigen, der es bedacht: also entstehen auch alle
hro aus diesem einzigen Dinge, durch Ordnung der Natur.   Sein Vater ist die Sonne, und seine Mutter der W
uft trägt es gleich als in ihrer Gebährmutter; Seine Ernährerin oder Säugamme ist die Erde.   Dies Ding
ng aller Vollkommenheiten so in der Welt sind. Seine Kraft ist am vollkommensten wann es wieder in Erde verm
Scheide alsdann die Erde vom Feuer, und das Subtile oder Dünne vom Dicken oder Groben, sein lieblich mit
nd und Bescheidenheit.   Es steigt von der Erde gen Himmel, und von dannen wiederum zur Erde, und nimmt a
aft des Obern und Untern.   Also wirst du haben die Herrlichkeit der ganzen Welt.   Derohalben weiche von die

Die Occulten Figuren der Rosenkreutzer *(p. 17)*. Tabula Smaragdina
Hermetis *dedicated to Hermes. See p. 33.*

Die Geheimen Figuren der Rosenkreutzer (p. 34, detail), above right of the
bunches of grapes (connected to the picture of a sword, a snake and a chalice) a
verse reads: 'I am the image of God and through the wine have fallen into death and
come to life again through it'. See p. 77.

DE

MERCVRIVS ☿ MERCVRIO

Per Sal, Sulphur, Mercurium
Fit Lapis Philosophorum.

A

TINCTU ALPHA ET OMEGA VITÆ SPES ES POST MORTEM ♃ REVIVIFICATIO
IHS

Geminæ
& Maternæ
Verg. lib. 6.
Mundi fundum
laborando
crede mihi
unde beari.

Columbæ
Aves.
Æneidi
si profundum
in veneris
habes totum
poteris.

Durch ☉ ♀ ☿ ist unser Anfang des Lebens,
und alle Dinge, NB. auch das Ende alles
Bösen, und nach der Fäulung dessen eine neue
Geburt, welche besser als vorher gewesen.

O

O UNICUS AMOR DEI IN TRINITATE MISERERE MEI IN ÆTERNITATE

Du Anfang und Ende des Lebens
Die Hoffnung bistu nach dem Tod.
Saturnus die Wiedergeburht,
Sol, Luna, derselben Leib

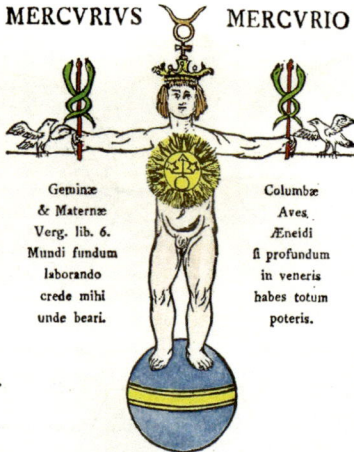

O! Einzige Liebe Gottes in der
Dreyfaltigkeit, erbarme dich mei-
ner in Ewigkeit.

Der Thau des Himmels und die Fettigkeit der Erden ist unser Kunst-Subjectum oder Materia. Es ist also weder Mineral noch Metall; das Pytagori-

sche Y zeiget uns, daß es zwey mercurialische Substantien sind einer Wurzel, Feuer und Wasser, Ischschamaim, nemlich ☿ gezogen aus der Minera

darinnen alle Metalle und Mineren liegen. Es ist ein ☉ Thau des Himmels, aber ein Mineral- und Metallischen Thau des Himmels, darinnen alle Farben der Welt liegen, welcher mag durch Kunst coaguliret werden in ein süsses Salz, Manna genannt, zur Arzeney; Sol Pater, Luna Mater, aus diesen
beyden empfängt er sein Licht, Leben und Glanz, aus der Sonnen sein feuriges, aus der Luna sein wässeriges Lichtwesen. Wir finden ihn coaguliret
und sölviret. Dieser Thau fällt von oben in die Tiefe der Erden, und von dem subtilesten Theil der Erden ist sein Körper, von oben kömmt seine Seele
und Geist, Feuer und Licht, und gehet in einen salzigen Leib, und empfängt die Kräffte (nempe Virtutes Substantiales) der obern und untern Dinge.
Unsern Augen erscheinet dieser Mineral-Thau an Farben weiß, gelb, grün, roth und schwarz, mehr Farben hat er den äussern Augen nach nicht. Denn er
erscheinet den äussern Augen corporalisch; in den Bergen wird er von den Bergleuten zuweilen gesehen, den äussern Augen nach dick, wässerig-abtrieffend,
aber weder ihnen noch den Künstlern nütze, sintemalen man nicht weissen kann, wozu er von der Natur ordiniret worden auf ein Mineral oder Metall,
und auf welches Geschlecht, das ist unwissend und unerkenntlich. Der beste ist, der coagulirte wie ein Electrum, oder wie der durchsichtige Bernstein, an
der Farbe als gemeldet. Ich weis nicht wozu in die Welt brauche, und er ist doch mit seinen Kräfften in allen Dingen. Er selbst aber ist von ihnen
veracht und verworfen; er scheidet sich in zwey Aeste, weiß und roth, aus der einigen Wurzel Y, und er stehet auf der einigen Wurzel da er wächst, wie
eine weisse und rothe Rose von Jericho, und blühet wie eine Lilie im Thal Josaphat stehende; von den Bergmann vielmal unzeitig abgebrochen, von uns
verständigen Arbeitern gemartert. Der rechte Künstler merkt seine Influenz, und bricht ihn selbst in seiner Reise, mit Blüthe, Saamen, Wurzel, Stamm
und Zweigen, nemlich in der Reise durchs Gesicht der innern geöffneten Augen. Dies sey genug von seiner körperlichen Gestalt; er ist kein Metall noch
Mineral, und doch aller Metallen und Mineren anfängliche Mutter und erste Materia.

Es ist nichts als der Löwe mit seinem coagulirten Blut, und das Gluten des weissen Adlers.

Wer es suchet der leibe,
Wer es find der schweige,
Wer es hat der verberge es,
Wer es brauchet der thue es unbekannt.
Wer ein wahrer Philosophus ist
Der bleibe ungenannt,
Traue niemand als Gott,
Der allein hält sein Wort,
Deines Gemüths Freund erwehlen sollt,
Sey mit jedermann freundlich,
Traue aber niemand,
Sey niemand geheim als Gott,
Willt du nicht betrogen seyn.
Experto crede Ruberto.

Denn Treue ist von der Erden gen Himmel geflogen, hat alle Menschen verlassen, deren Gemüth an der Erden klebet.

Die Geheimen Figuren der Rosenkreutzer *(p. 48), 'The dew of heaven and the fatness of the earth. . .'. See p. 53.*

realm to which in its way today's more materialistic thinking leads [written in 1931] when 'vitamins' are mentioned as something chemically incalculable, something in our food that cannot be reduced to a chemical formula. An important border-region between the chemical and the chymical realm opens up at this point. Does it have to remain in the future forever closed to the human spirit?

That which in the *wine of the Marriage at Cana* as the *chymical mystery of the Earth's future* is prophetically placed by Christ before people; then in the Mystery of Golgotha, in the blood streaming from the wounds of the Crucified that sinks directly into the Earth, it becomes the seed for this future. In Christ's blood starry forces of cosmic life give themselves to the dying Earth. Nowhere do we feel so close to the mystery of the *red tincture* and its power to metamorphose the earthly, material world, than in the Mystery of the Blood of Golgotha. It appears in the Manichean picture of the self-sacrifice of the *tincture of light* (JG, p. 388, p. 407, *etc.*), sacrificing itself into the darkness of the earthly element, also repeatedly mentioned by Jakob Böhme.[64] Rudolf Steiner has shown how, for the clairvoyant vision, the Earth started to shine as in a new starry light, began to shine as a star amongst stars when it received the seed of the Sun of the future, the seed of its own Sun-becoming (JG, p. 387ff.). Rudolf Steiner expressed the conviction (Lecture, Berlin. 25 March 1907. GA 96; and similarly in *From Jesus to Christ*. Lecture 4, Karlsruhe. 8 Oct. 1911. GA 131) that nobody has come exoterically closer to this esoteric (chymical-esoteric) mystery than Richard Wagner in his music drama *Parsifal*. In modern times this has for the first time been placed before humanity. And what was presented above (Chapters 2 and 3) of the connections of the *chymical* and of the *musical element* is nowhere to be experienced so directly as in Wagner's *Parsifal*. Already at the end of the Prelude and then again in Acts 1 and 2, in the vision of Amfortas and of Parsifal, the glowing of the sacred Blood is spoken of in their beholding the Grail. Something like starlight twinkling within streaming blood, of 'blood turning itself into ether' (Steiner's expression) is eloquently expressed in the instrumental music. (On this, see the author's *The Parsifal=Christ=Experience in Wagner's Music Drama*).[65] At this point the chymical mystery becomes the Mystery of the Holy Grail.

The event of the streaming of water and blood out of the wounded side of the One crucified (John 19:34), at first seemingly not something unusual, is yet presented in the Gospel itself (John 19:35) as something like a Mystery. Contrary to other interpretations, here there appears to be an indication that the chymical motif of the Marriage of Cana is to be read between the lines. This is discussed in the author's book on John's Gospel [JG, p. 406ff.]. This is indicated also in the important parallel passage 1 John 5:6–8, where the elements of the Earth themselves are called as witnesses of the event, and details are given.

From here, we turn our attention once again to the mystery of the Marriage at Cana. This marriage appears in the Mystery-chapters of John's Gospel (John 1–5) like a tremendous prophecy of the future. The ruling constellation standing over the chapter — as could be shown in the author's exposition on John's Gospel (JG, 188ff.) — directly indicates this prophecy of the future, the chymical mystery of the chapter and of John's Gospel in general. In this constellation the Saturn-Uranus sign of the Waterman links to the Sun-sign of the Lion. The two water jars of the Waterman signify here, as do the water jars (baptism jars) at the 'Marriage in Cana' itself — as does 'water' generally regarding the substance metamorphosed here through the strength of Christ — the mystery of the primal water and of the still non-personalized etheric [element]. The Lion signifies Christ's Sun-ego-strength, that works here as the One who metamorphoses.

In the planetary aspect of the Waterman, there still lies a significant mystery for the prophecy of the chapter, as well as for everything chymical. Here as the ruler of the Waterman we find Saturn, that points towards everything coming from *below*, from the Earth, which carries earthly strength and earthly weight in itself. But in addition to this, we find Uranus, which, as boundary-marker and cosmic boundary-stone of Uranos, the upper starry heaven, of the 'crystal heaven' beyond Saturn, points towards *that which comes from above*. (In Uranos-Saturn the polarity 'heaven and earth' is mirrored cosmically.) What comes from above carries in itself the crystal forces of the cosmos, trans-forming the Earth, building anew the earthly body into the temple of the future. In alchymy this was also called 'the crystal-bright philoso-pher's stone'. It was venerated in the 'heavenly salt', of which the salt-cube is the earthly picture (whereby in Rev. 21:16, the cube-form of the New Jerusalem, was glimpsed). Here we particularly recall what was developed earlier (Chapter 2) on the chymical mystery of the process of nourishment with the reference to John 6:51.

Thus there also lies in the Waterman, inasmuch as it is a Uranus-sign, a chymical mystery of the future. In the last lecture of the cycle *Between Death and Rebirth* (Berlin 5 Nov. 1912–1 April 1913. GA 141), Rudolf Steiner shows how the Uranos-power beyond Saturn (♒ ♅) building up the new earthly body, is connected with Christ's Sun-soul power in the Lion, in the heart (☉ ♌) through the birth of the soul of the Earth through the Mystery of Golgotha. Steiner himself speaks in the first lecture-cycle on *The Gospel of St John* [Hamburg 1908. GA 103], indicating how the prophecy contained in the chapter on Cana ('and on the *third day* there was a wedding in Cana of Galilee') is related to the great wedding of humanity (the 'chymical wedding') in the future (sixth post-Atlantean) cultural epoch, or in the transitional period leading up to it. (The mystery-experiences of the 'first day' had to do with the fourth, of the 'second day' with the fifth, and those experiences of the 'third day' had to do with the sixth cultural epoch).

This transitional period is at the same time the Waterman-Uranus age (spring equinox of the Sun in ♒) whose beginning, purely astronomically, is no longer far distant. In the Uranus-sign of the Waterman standing over the chapter [John 2] there also lie references to these ages. Not without deeper meaning, the first chapters of John's Gospel follow the 'great cosmic [Platonic] year' resulting from the precession of the spring equinox (more details in the author's exposition on John's Gospel). For the astrological and chymical world-knowledge, this future age will be a new era. Only then will the true meaning of the wedding-mystery at Cana be revealed to human consciousness. The chymical mystery of the Christ-future lying between ♒ ⚷ ♅ and ☉ ♌ will then be revealed:

> One day the stars, down dripping,
> Shall flow in golden wine:
> We, of that nectar sipping,
> As living stars will shine.
> (Novalis, from *Hymns to the Night*. Tr. George MacDonald.)

The word Uranos itself, via the Indian Váruṇa (the god of the nightly heavens and of the waters of the sea), is related to *Urna* 'urn' (or the two urns) of the Waterman. Once again the context of the Greek Uranos-myth appears. The water jars of the Marriage at Cana have already been mentioned. The mystery of the water urns links to that of the urns for human ashes. It is deeply significant how in the final chapter entitled 'Cana in Galilee' of Book 7 of his great novel *The Brothers Karamazov*, Dostoyevsky, the Russian novelist, strongly feeling the future-prophecy of the Cana-chapter, connects the mystery of Cana with the mystery of the entombment, with the experiences at the coffin of a beloved person (JG, p. 201f.). In John's Gospel itself the constellation of Cana reappears with the entombment of Christ, as before in the constellation of Lazarus, whose mysteries Dostoyevsky wove in such a unique way into his narration (JG, p. 342f.). And this connection of Uranos (heaven) and the 'urn of the dead' (urn containing the ashes) brings before our soul the saying of Novalis (mentioned above in Chapter 3) in connection with the chymical mysteries of ashes and sulphur: 'All ash is pollen; the [flower] chalice is heaven.' Thus in the Waterman Uranus-sign the chymical mystery of water (Mercury) is connected with the mystery of ash-sulphur.

Where — one would like to ask — is the third of the three chymical principles, the salt (*sal*)? After all that we hitherto could present, is not *Uranos* itself the living light-salt (*Licht-Salz*) of the heavenly forces that build up and resurrect? (if we are allowed to use the expression quite common with the alchymists). The 'living light-salt', the 'heavenly salt', finds its earthly counter-picture in the dead, earthly salt of the sea (think of the 'Dead Sea', the salt-sea). In alchymical literature (for example, in the *Der Rosenkreutzer*, p. 46 [p. 304], also in the baptism verse, quoted here p. 57 and in the present author's *Our Origin in the Light*) this contrast of the living and the dead, of the heavenly and the earthly salt, is everywhere mentioned. Through all this the myth of Uranos, already discussed in the light of the three chymical principles, receives a yet deeper meaning when we become aware how the starry semen of Uranos, fallen into the cosmic ocean (the heavenly light-salt) out of which Venus-Aphrodite arises, finds its earthly counter-picture in the salty element of the sea.

The constellation of the 'Marriage at Cana' (♒ — ♌) tells us how Christ's 'I'-power of the Sun in the Lion, in the heart

> (... the stars, down dripping,
> Shall flow in golden wine ...)

unites with the upbuilding forces for the new earthly body, with the heavenly forces of Uranos that build up, of the living Uranian light-salt symbolized in the salt-cube crystalline form of the 'New Jerusalem' of the Apocalypse. All these things are not dragged in, for John's Gospel itself speaks of them. In John 2, the mystery of Cana is united with the apparently remote subject, the rebuilding of the ruined Temple (John 2:19), which is explained as the temple of the body (John 2:21). The detailed connections, including the historical context, are discussed in JG, p. 201 (also MG. p. 250ff.). Here the point is to show, in the light of the Uranos-sign of the Waterman, how the mystery of rebuilding the

Temple, linked with that of the 'New Jerusalem' as the metamorphosed Earth, the new earthly body, can be understood through the mystery of Cana.

With regard to the 'mysteries of wine' (☉ ♌) with the Marriage at Cana, in addition to the saying of Novalis concerning the 'new wine of life', one can say that they did play a role in alchymy in general. Amongst other things, wine belongs to the chymically significant substances.[66] In *Die Geheimen Figuren der Rosenkreutzer*, p. 34 [p. 278], behind [that is, just above and to the right] the picture of the bunches of grapes (connected to the picture of a sword, a snake and a chalice) a remarkable verse is found: 'I am the image of God, through wine I fell into death and through wine I came back again to life.' Many things that Rudolf Steiner says in his lecture-cycles on the Marriage in Cana, especially on the historical mission of wine (in the positive and negative sense), wonderfully illuminate the depths of this Rosicrucian saying.

The mystery of bread and wine of the Last Supper relating to the metamorphosis, the transubstantiation of the Earth, is to be considered here. In the Gospel—in John and in Mark—this mystery stands in the sign of the Virgin, regarding which, as we know, it is the sign of the mystery of the Earth ('the activity of the stars in earthly matter'), the sign of alchymy. It is governed by Mercury, who, with the other co-governors Saturn and Venus, clearly stands related to the chymical mystery of the Earth. As with the Waterman alongside Saturn-Uranus, so also with the Virgin (alongside Mercury-Venus, who are co-governors in the Waterman), the earthly Saturn is alone emphasized. Consequently, the chymical aspect with the sign of the Virgin is again a different one than with the constellation Waterman-Lion. The Virgin is more an earth-sign; the constellation Waterman-Lion indicates more the heavenly renewal of the Earth.

In John 6, in Christ's proclamation of the 'flesh and blood of the "I"' (John 6:54, 55), the Last-Supper mysteries of bread and wine appear with the strongest emphasis of the 'I'-viewpoint in conjunction with the metamorphosis of the earthly and the building-up of the new earthly body ('I am the bread of life/living bread which came down from heaven', John 6:51) and in a remarkable connection with the mystery of the *manna* (John 6:31 & 49), that always includes the motif of 'star-activity in earthly matter'. In this case—with the 'manna in the desert' of the Hebrews—it concerns the decadent remnant of a once 'cosmic distribution', of the 'bread of the stars'.

The motif of the 'new source of life' in John 4, in the meeting of Christ with the woman of Samaria at the well, is closely related to the mystery of the blood of Golgotha. The old, dried up source of life is replaced with the source coming to life within the 'I', the 'spring of water welling up to eternal life — to the life of the aeons, of future time' [John 4:14]. (For further details on the contexts, see the author's JG. p. 219ff., especially 225ff.) All this calls before the soul the motif of the Paradisal stream — now renewed in the Mystery of Golgotha — whose chymical mysteries were discussed above (Chapter 3). The motif of John 4 reappears chymically intensified as the 'I'-motif in John 7:38: 'He who believes in me' — that is, 'whoever allows the "I" to become strong in himself' (Latin *pistis* 'faith' is related to the German *fest* 'firm') — 'from his heart shall flow rivers of living water.' In passing, John 3, the Nicodemus chapter, is to be considered, whose motif of being 'born from above' climaxes in the *mystery of the wind of life, which blows down from cosmic heights* (JG, p. 213). All this lies in the direction of the chymical mystery of breathing, discussed above ('work with the philosopher's stone'); it contains a motif which the alchymists have always claimed for themselves.

*   *   *

We recall that with the Mystery of Cana, with the water freshly drawn out of the earthly spring, it depended on the fact that Christ 'was the being Who had just approached the Earth; He had just become acquainted with the forces that work in the Earth itself' (R. Steiner. *The Gospel of St John in Relation to the Three Other Gospels*, Lecture 9. GA 112). This motif, also to be heard in a certain manner in John 8 (JG. p. 293), appears in a chymical intensification in John 9, where, by uniting the substance of his own body with that of the Earth (John 9:6), Christ opens the eyes of the man born blind. Already here, we sense Christ unites with the Earth; increasingly He relates to her with the substance of His own body; increasingly the *tincture of the light* is sacrificed into the darkness of the earthly realm; increasingly the tincture releases into earthly decay the forces of the light that stand in a mysterious relationship to the 'mysteries of decay' in general (JG, p. 301ff.). One could speak of it in an alchymical, technical manner, how here through Christ the *materia ultima* (the end-condition, or state of decay of matter) is brought close to its initial condition, to the *materia prima*.

This whole relating of Christ to the depths of death of the Earth leads to a still higher chymical intensification in the Mystery of Bethany, in the *raising of Lazarus*, until it finds its crowning conclusion in the Mystery of Golgotha itself. The *Mystery of Bethany*, as it could be shown in the *John's Gospel: the Cosmic Rhythm*, is itself actually the beginning of the *Mystery of Golgotha*, to which the *Mystery of Cana* points as in a picture. It is only the sacrificial, divine Love sacrificing itself in the dying of Christ into the darkness of the Earth as the tincture of the light, the seed of the light in the earthly grave, that is able to tear away the enclosed bodily sheaths of Lazarus, already in the grip of the forces of decay. And it is only the 'disciple whom the Lord loved' who can open himself completely as a chalice to receive this divine Love, Christ's Love as a direct *life-awakening Love*. These, too, are mysteries of *Venus Urania*. The saying of Novalis, so deeply moved by the Johannine spirit, 'Love is the basis of the possibility of magic; love is magically active',[67] discovers here its highest chymical manifestation. Further details on these connections can be found in JG (p. 341ff., especially 345ff.): 'The raising of Lazarus is wrested from the death of Christ.'

The raising of Lazarus was seen by the alchymists as an exalted uplifting into the highest cosmic-earthly, historical event, a divine fulfilment of their 'chymical process'. They stood before it as a picture where in their own way they experienced and presented the transition through the forces of dying and of decay and then to the process of re-enlivening and resurrecting in the realm of matter. We recall the degrees of the chymical process discussed with the biblical story of Noah [Chapter 3], of the

- 'Mortification' (killing) and
- 'Putrefaction' (bringing matter closer to the forces of decay) as far as
- 'Dissolution' (in the case of Lazarus, that would be the breaking of the bonds of the grave through the word of Christ Jesus, the word that has in itself the power of the sound-ether, which in union with the life-ether are at the same time the 'chymical forces'),
- 'Re-enlivening',
- ['Purifying',]
- 'Fulfilment' and
- 'Re-awakening' (*Resuscitatio*, as this final degree is also called in alchymical writings).

All this passes before us in the raising of Lazarus from an unbounded, elevated viewpoint. And we can well understand, when we bring to consciousness the now often-presented relationship of the Lazarus-event to the initiation of John (JG, p. 319ff.), how the disciple John —

claimed by the alchymists as one of themselves — through these events of the most central chymical mystery was certainly in his deep, most inner being moved and gripped. He could then express the chymical motif, which was already revealed so significantly in the Mystery of Cana, in his Gospel, in its world-historic, unique greatness.

The actual conclusion and crowning climax of this chymical context of John's Gospel lies in the *Mystery of Golgotha* itself, already mentioned at the beginning of this section. Here in what happens to the blood on the cross, the Earth-mysteries of John's Gospel and the mysteries of the stars meet in the deepest manner. In the *entombment of Christ Jesus* is revealed the most significant of all the parallels displaying the [cosmic] rhythm of the Gospel (JG, p. 333), between the Mystery of Lazarus, the 'grave of Bethany', and the Mystery of Golgotha itself. In looking at the Mystery of Bethany, at the story of Lazarus, we can intuit how far, too, in the entombment of Christ (in its connection to the resurrection) most profound chymical mysteries are hidden.

A chymical motif that cannot be overlooked apparently lies already in what is said (John 19:37–40) about the embalming of the body of Jesus with certain aromatic substances through Joseph of Arimathea and Nicodemus, both of whom we take as standing in an esoteric relationship to Christ and the group of disciples (JG, p. 208). Steiner, too, has suggested these things as a cause for the quick dissolution of the corpse, with the addition of another connection.[68] The decisive thing with these processes, of course, is the fact that it was the bodily vessel taken up by the cosmic Christ, which at that time like a *chymical seed, a grain of wheat*, was entrusted to the depths of the Earth. The connection of these *mysteries of the seed, of the grain of wheat*, always to be conceived in the alchymical sign of the Virgin, already sounds so profoundly in the Greek mysteries of Eleusis. John's Gospel itself emphasizes Christ's deed for the Earth on Golgotha in the verse (John 12:24): 'Truly, truly, I say to you, unless a grain of wheat falls into the earth and dies, it remains alone; but if it dies, it bears much fruit.'

Another picture for the mystery of the entombment and resurrection that sees the resurrection-body in the apocalyptic picture, appearing already in the Wedding in Cana (John 2:19–21), the picture of the resurrection temple and the future temple of the 'New Jerusalem', is echoed in the saying of Novalis: '... who has laid Himself into the Earth to become a *foundation-stone of a City of God*' [*Spiritual Songs*, 12]. With the alchymists we find a similar meaning in the saying *Christ the cornerstone*, which they use for their 'philosopher's stone' with special reference to Psalm 118:22 and Luke 20:18 (*Figuren der Rosenkreutzer*, p. 51 [p. 314]). The sum content of the connections existing here in reality can become clear from the whole discussion.

In the entombment of Christ, too, as in the events of Cana, the mysteries of Saturn unite with those of Uranus in the sign of the Waterman (JG, p. 409ff.). In no other passage of the Gospel do *earthly mystery* and *star-mystery* resonate together as with the events of this sign governed by Saturn and Uranus. The earthly forces unite with Saturn, the starry forces with Uranus. 'Heaven and earth' are united in the activity of both [wandering] stars. This differentiates the sign of the Waterman, bright and relieved of the weight of earth—astrologically it is an 'air-sign' and 'light-ether sign'—from the weight of the dark earth-sign of the Goat, governed alone by Saturn. This sign of the Waterman, bright and relieved of the weight of earth, in contrast to the earlier 'darkness at the cross', to be conceived in the Saturn-sign of the Goat, is the perceptible mood pouring over the whole narration of the Gospel from the entombment of Christ (John 19:38–42). We recall here the '*Lösung*—dissolution' (*Solutio*) in the 'chymical process'. Here, too, there lies a mystery of heavenly love, *Venus Urania* (Novalis: 'The resolving hand (*lösende Hand*) of Eternal Love came, and he fell asleep in death.' [*Hymns to the Night*, 5])

In this way, *earthly mystery* and *star-mystery* meet in the entombment of Christ. It is like a communing of earthly depths and starry heights concerning the resurrection-future of both the Earth and of humanity that takes place over Christ's entombment and over the mystery of burial in general. Goethe's words:

> The stars on high are silent still;
> Silent the graves, nor make reply

we repeatedly recall in this connection. Furthermore, what Dostoyevsky in his chapter 'Cana in Galilee' [in *The Brothers Karamazov*] writes (JG, p. 203): 'The silence of earth seemed to melt into the silence of the heavens. *The mystery of earth was one with the mystery of the stars....*'

How far in this meeting of starry heights and earthly depths there really lies a *chymical motif* shines out of the whole discussion. It should still be pointed out how this motif lived as a mood in Novalis, to whom we could frequently refer as a witness of the Johannine spirit. With Novalis, we find this in the chymical mood of dialogue between the starry heights and the earthly depths, especially in the remarkable miners' Chapter 5 in *Heinrich von Ofterdingen*, where at one place the hermit under the earth speaks these words to the visiting miner:

> 'You miners are well nigh inverted astrologers,' said the hermit; 'as they ceaselessly regard the sky, wandering through its immeasurable spaces, so do you turn your gaze to the earth, exploring its construction. Astrologers study the forces and influences of the stars, while you are discovering the forces of rocks and mountains, and the various properties of earth and stone strata. To them the higher world is a book of futurity; to you the earth is a memorial of the primeval world.'

Here we also find emphasized the cosmogonic motif of alchymy.

Goethe, too, includes this connection of astrological with chymical motifs in his novel *Wilhelm Meister's Apprenticeship* that contains deep mysteries. Here there is the mysterious, starry transfigured character of Makarien, in whom a sacred astrology is essentially incorporated, so that in her loosely grounded soul-organism she can follow the planetary courses in their rhythmical dances in the cosmic distances, in order to bring what was experienced there as moral impulses into earthly life. And on the other side is 'she who feels the metals', the friend of Montan, who in a similar manner, only in the opposite direction, senses the mysteries of the earthly depths. In a lecture held in Dornach (7 July 1923. GA 225), Rudolf Steiner points to the mystery of both these personalities in its relationship to the threefold human being. He shows how in the 'balance of astrology upwards and alchymy downwards true humanity is to be found', and how for ages amongst artisans there were individual 'diviners', who contemplating such contexts could tell people about them, indeed, that such 'diviners' were useful precisely for specific practical professional tasks, for instance, to find springs and to construct wells. This usefulness was also recognized by their colleagues, was valued and put to practical use.

*   *   *

The Revelation of John

The *event of the resurrection* stands already in a clearly perceptible 'chymical' connection with the mystery of the Entombment. Its beginning is contained in the opening of the final two chapters of John's Gospel, and concludes in the 'Revelation of John'. There the resurrection-experience appears in its complete fullness. The whole content of the Apocalypse *is* this experience of resurrection, the appearance and revelation of the living Christ in His resurrected form, uniting Himself with the physically resurrected Earth, changing and renewing her through all the crises of her evolution into a chymically exalted and transfigured form. Like that which we called the 'starry meaning' and the 'material meaning', the 'chymical' meaning of the Bible, especially recognized in the opening cosmogonic chapters but later more receding, appears ever more strongly in the Apocalypse towards the end. Novalis, everywhere moved by the Johannine chymical spirit recognized, and in his *Fragments* expresses, how the beginning and end of the Bible, Paradise and the 'New Jerusalem', inwardly meet. And more clearly than anything else, he allows the 'chymical' viewpoint to be recognized with the much discussed and disputed relationship between John's Gospel and the Apocalypse, and the lines of connection between them. However the outer documents and historical philological studies are able to judge this connection, for the spiritual viewpoint — and precisely where this spiritual viewpoint has taken into itself the chymical aspect — the connection is surely present.

With all this we are dealing not only with the 'chymical motifs' of the Apocalypse, as they met us right at the beginning [of this book] in the 'philosopher's stone' connected with the 'activity of the stars in earthly matter', but, moreover, with the decisive link for the Christian era of the 'stone' with the human 'I'. For nothing other than the 'crystal bright philosopher's stone', the bright resurrection-substance, the 'light-earth' of the New Jerusalem is the 'white stone'; nothing other than the 'activity of the stars in earthly matter', the new reception of the influence of the stars in the 'I' as heavenly nourishment, the building-up and experience of new corporeality through the power of the upper star-forces is meant with the 'hidden manna'; the 'new name, which no one knows except he who receives it' is again none other than the name 'I'. Rev. 2:17:

> To him who conquers I will give some of the hidden manna, and I will give him a white stone, with a new name written on the stone which no one knows except him who receives it.

Compare here, Rev. 3:12:

> He who conquers, I will make him a pillar in the temple of my God: never shall he go out of it, and I will write on him the name of my God, and the name of the city of my God, the new Jerusalem which comes down from my God out of heaven, and my own new name, the name 'I'.

Alongside essential motifs of the new star-wisdom (Rev. 1:16 & 20; see also JG, pp. 154–56), of the astrology of the 'I', in the Apocalypse we find essential motifs of the new wisdom of earthly matter (the alchymy of the 'I'). But not only these individual motifs come now into consideration. For, from the given starting point of this contemplation, *the whole Apocalypse contains*, in a grandiose unfolding and intensification, from the 'seven letters' via the 'seven seals' and the 'seven trumpets' right to the 'seven bowls of wrath' and the final transfiguration and fulfilment in the 'heavenly Earth' of the New Jerusalem and of the new Paradise garden, *nothing other than a single great chymical process* on a colossal cosmic scale. No longer are we dealing with the destiny of some sort of fragments of matter, the formation of earthly matter, but with the destiny of the entire Earth, with the reforming of the whole of Earth-existence, right into the depths of matter, right through unheard-of crises of evolution, under ever new, always more fearful and more agonising birth-pains.

Here a terrible struggle of the elements of darkness against the elements of light will be unleashed, until in this great division, in this 'crisis', everything will be revealed that strives against the light. In this struggle all the counter-forces exhaust the might of their assault until right through all these crises, the 'fundamental change' of the earthly is finally accomplished. Now, from above, the new connection, the penetration of the (Saturnian) darkness of Earth with the Uranian powers of light from the upper world, from the 'heavenly' realm, can come about.

Earthly evolution itself, by its standing right within cosmic-evolution, *passes before us in this apocalyptic description as a great chymical process.* This is not only pictorially expressed, but is in harmony with the fundamental chymical tenet, 'As above, so below; as below, so above.' It is really meant that this great process in the development of the Earth and the dramatic process of the Earth's smelting in actual fact presents in cosmically enlarged proportions that which takes place in detail under the hands of the *genuine* alchymists as a drama of matter, as the dramatic formation of matter through all possible crises, dangers and new formations. Every earthly formation of matter, every genuine 'chymical process' is the reduced picture of the great chymical-apocalyptic process of the Earth. What 'material', what matter really is, what it contains in itself for the darknesses and poison opposed to life, for demonic forces of lightning, for super-earthly revelations of light, is unimaginable for daytime consciousness; it is experienced only by those in real observation, in serious devoted attempts in these realms of facts, from the beginning of the chemical right to the hidden heights and backgrounds of the chymical, penetrating ever further from degree to degree, who find the key to their mysteries.

Thus each higher earthly forming of matter, each genuine 'chymical process' would really be the smaller picture of the great chymical and apocalyptic process of the Earth. That we are dealing here not only with outer technical matters but with spiritual matters has been sufficiently emphasized. Whoever today would be a real expert of chymical processes in their technical details would certainly have to enter into the subject and show in the smallest details how between the lines of the Apocalypse an exact description of the chymical process, all its critical events and dramatic moments are hidden, even if indecipherable to the non-initiate. Precisely that which appears in the Apocalypse, for example, with the opening of the seal, with the sounding of the trumpets, with the pouring out of the bowls of wrath as horrors, would really be the exact counter-picture of what is experienced in the genuine chymical process with the drama of matter in formation as horrors and episodes, crises and dangers.

With all this it is really not intended that the Apocalypse would merely be an 'alchymical' document, where in obscure cosmic pictures chymical processes are so described that only the initiate and those technically experienced in alchymy can find their way (which was normal in alchymical literature), this is sufficiently evident from the whole exposition up to now. But, as has been clearly stated, the Apocalypse really does have to do with a description of the future destinies of mankind and the Earth. Yet just as this is true, the other is true as well, that the destinies and processes of the chymical drama of matter are a smaller picture of the great drama of the Earth, as seen by the clairvoyant eye of the Apocalyptist, of 'John the alchymist', seen and presented in a grandiose manner in the conclusion of the New Testament, the Apocalypse crowning the Gospels.

From the previous contemplation and from the descriptions of the alchymists we know how in the chymical process, when it did work (which occurred seldom and only experienced by a very few) and its successful ending was approaching, a rainbow phenomenon formed, a colour-experience showed itself, in which the scale of the rainbow colours was manifested. In the Apocalypse the same rainbow phenomenon is there in cosmic proportions, where after all the crises and horrors have been fought through, and death has been excluded from the progressive evolution (Rev. 20:14; the corresponding stage in the chymical process would be the *caput mortuum*, the 'raven's head'), but the New Jerusalem in a river of gold comes down out of the upper, Uranian world. The *twelve precious stones* are described, with which the foundations of the walls of the Holy City are adorned.

In comparing these twelve jewels according to their colours, one finds there are five dark, that is, opaque, and seven bright jewels, that is, such with transparent colours.[*] If we leave the five opaque stones initially out of account, whose colours are also considerably varied and indistinct, the seven bright stones that remain in fact show the series of the colours of the rainbow, as follows: The first bright stone to be described, the *sapphire* (for the first named stone jasper is opaque red) reveals the *blue*, followed by *green* and *yellow* (topaz) to *red* ('jacinth' — is not the red corundum, the *ruby*, meant?), and the *violet* in the *amethyst* is the last. In order to form an image, one has to think of twelve stones (or colours) arranged in a circle. The rainbow is also based on this colour-circle, whereby we can imagine that the visible bow of the seven bright colours is supplemented into a complete circle of twelve through the invisible bow of the five 'ultra-colours'. In this colour-circle, for example, opposite to *green* stands the '*peach-blossom*', as it does in Goethe's colour-circle. With the apocalyptic bow of colours (or colour-circle) it is the case that the colours lying outside the septenary, or precious stones (chalcedony, sardonyx, sardius, chrysoprase, jasper), are distributed amongst the others, and that we do not have between red and yellow the transition colour orange, nor between blue and violet the transition colour indigo, but rather the *green* is divided into three colour-nuances (*emerald* deep green, *chrysolite* green, *beryl* yellow green), and in this way it plays an especially important role. Together with peach-blossom lying opposite, green is the 'mediating colour'. The actual colour, corresponding to the spirit of Christ: in green and peach-blossom we experience something like the balance of the polarity of colours.

Obviously, the apocalyptic precious-stone colour-circle also carries in itself the zodiac, the arrangement of the twelve sacred, heavenly signs. As the cardinal axis (traverse axis), it possesses with the pre-sentation of the Gospel [cosmic] rhythm, the zodiacal axis, which is always called the 'Last Supper constellation' ♓ — ♍ (♓ jasper, ♍

---

[*] In his works on tonality, Beckh describes the musical keys as five darker and seven brighter keys — *Tr. note.*

chrysolite), whereby ♓ is the sign of the beginning of the Christ-events[*], the Christ-sign of the present cultural epoch, or of the Christ-era beginning with the Baptism in the Jordon, the sign of the Sun-power of Christ's 'I'. Then in this contemplation we have recognized in ♍ the 'alchymical sign', the sign of the Mystery of the Earth ('the activity of the stars in earthly matter'), so that this cardinal axis of the colour-circle, in the way it connects the sign of alchymy with the sign of the Christ-'I', quite clearly points towards the new Christ-alchymy, the alchymy of the 'I'.

For the further description of the apocalyptic jewels and their colours according to the zodiac we have to accept that the order given in Rev. 21:19 & 20 is not the usual sequence (♓ ♈ ♉ ♊, *etc.*), the order that lies at the basis of Mark's Gospel, but the Johannine sequence lying as the basis of the cosmic rhythm of John's Gospel (JG, p. 73ff.). The movement there is not in the seasonal course through the bright sounds upwards,[†] but the opposite direction of the great cosmic [Platonic] year via the dark signs downwards, that is, the order ♓ ♒ ♑ ♐ *etc.* On the actual cardinal sign of the zodiac, at the Uranus-sign, ♒ which we ascribed to the Marriage at Cana and the Entombment, we meet the light-filled blue *sapphire* — the light blue belonging to Uranos, 'heaven', the sky — and from one point of view, which is at the same time the 'Uranus viewpoint', the sapphire is an exalted stone of Christ. (From another point of view, — not mentioned in the Apocalypse — tourmaline, which connects the light green with the peach-blossom, appears as the stone of Christ.[69]

- In the *sapphire* would consequently be seen a special elevated revelation of the divine, a future revelation [Waterman].
- The opaque blue *chalcedony* would then come in the 'dark Saturn sign' of the Goat,
- the deep green *emerald* in the Archer, the spring of the new stream of life (John 4; see also JG, p. 219ff.),
- the opaque varying red of *sardonyx* in the Scorpion,
- *sardius* (or *carnelion*) in the Scales,
- the light green *chrysolite* in the Virgin,
- *beryl* in the Lion,
- *topaz* in the Crab,
- *chrysoprase* in the Twins,
- *jacinth* in the Bull,

---

[*] See Beckh's studies on Mark and John — *Tr. note.*
[†] explored in the author's work on tonality — *Tr. note.*

- *amethyst* in the Ram, the day-bright sign of the clarity of consciousness (this meaning also lies in the Greek name ἀμέθυστος), [and
- *jasper*, in the Fishes.][70]

In all this the essential viewpoint for contemplation is that we can show the rainbow scale (with a certain characteristic emphasis on green) in this apocalyptic colour-scale of the precious stones, and with this the chymical phenomenon of the 'rainbow' is also demonstrated in the Apocalypse.

When in the Apocalypse the New Jerusalem, the city of the future of humanity, of the new transformed Earth descending out of heaven, is mentioned (Rev. 3:12, 21:2, 21:10), then this picture loses all its fairy-tale, fantastic character that seemingly surrounds it, when Rudolf Steiner shows (already mentioned above), how the building-up of the human body in nourishment, breathing and higher spiritual processes does not only occur through the usual earthly matter, but also how the finer forces are taken up in reverse direction, from above. Here, too, the Uranian, heavenly element appears in polar relationship to the earthly element. From the former there follows the construction of the 'New Jerusalem', of the resurrection body, of the metamorphosed, new higher physical body.

The mystery of the salt-cube form of the New Jerusalem (Rev. 21) was mentioned above. Here too lies a mystery of the 'Uranian light-earth', of the 'heavenly salt' of light. The upper part of the threefold human being also corresponds to the chymical 'salt' (*sal*), the nerve-sense organiza-tion that in fine, spiritual processes takes up the building-up forces from above. Here we stand again before the 'white stone', the 'crystal bright philosopher's stone', whose relationship to the three-dimensional forces of space contained in cubic form was mentioned above (Chapter 1). The 'space' of abstract thinking, as something flowing out to the periphery into infinity — or into 'nothing' — appears as an undefined sphere. The 'I', however, creatively fashions out of *nothing* (out of 'infinity') the forces of space into the temple-form of the cube and realises the cube as the 'building-thought'. From here the depths of the saying of Angelus Silesius gradually becomes apparent, which we have placed as a motto at the beginning of these contemplations:

The world appears round as a sphere,
that's why away it will pass,
The City of God is a cube,
that's why forever it stands fast.
[CW Book 4, 117]

In the *pearls* of the 'twelve gates' of the Holy City (Rev. 21:21) we can imagine transformed experiences of illness, transformed experiences of pain—for in this direction the mystery of the pearl always lies. The painful experiences and crises of suffering still to be penetrated, right up to the manifestation of the metamorphosed and transfigured 'new Earth', appear before our souls in this exalted picture. Now, *pearls belong to Venus*. We should not go amiss if we think here too of Botticelli's Venus, the *Venus Urania* of the Uranos-myth rising out of the seashell. Chymical mysteries of *Venus Urania* are revealed in the pearls and gates of pearl of the 'New Jerusalem'. They also gently indicate an Uranian element of the future Earth, mysteries of the Earth in the future. Significantly, this future of the Earth connects with the primal Paradisal past, where the original *garden* has now become the *city*, or more exactly expressed: to the etheric of the Paradise garden, the city has been added, built out of the 'I'-forces in the higher physical realm, descending from above: the pictures of the Tree of Life and the River of Life in Rev. 22 recall everything that we could discover in an earlier chapter of these contemplations in the pictures of the original paradise of the chymical mysteries of gold, of precious stones and of the chymical primal substance. And in the new Paradise garden bloom the flowers of the heavenly Venus, the 'eternal bloom and fruits' about which Novalis once spoke.[71] For him all the blooms and flowers of the earthly spring, children of the earthly Venus, are only an intimating parable. Thus the Mysteries of Venus, full of significance for all alchymy, are also woven into the apocalyptical description of the New Jerusalem.

Consequently there is a profound meaning in the final closing words of Christ in the Apocalypse, thereby ending the New Testament, and the Bible itself, in the actually closing words, Rev. 22:16 (for vv. 17–21 are an appendix), when we are so directed once more to this Venus mystery. Now Christ's 'I-AM' unites with the stars, whose dramatic destinies revealed in cosmic evolution are a reflection of the destiny of humanity, with the star of the Uranian mystery of heaven and the chymical mystery of the Earth. That star was once the noble jewel of the Grail, which in the fall of Lucifer-Phosphorus fell out of the crown of the Lord of Light. And now, itself a heavenly Grail, once again in divine purity and clarity in the Scales, the governing sign shines over the whole of John's Gospel, *Venus Urania*: '*I am* the root and the offspring of David, *the bright morning star*.'

Through Christ and the mysteries of the 'I', ancient star-knowledge has become again a *sacred astrology*, chymical knowledge of earthly matter a *sacred alchymy*. Moreover, when we add how in the name David and in the Psalms of David a Hebrew revelation of the Mercury Mysteries is contained, then we glimpse, alongside that which the 'root of David' signifies in a purely historical meaning, in the apocalyptic sense of these words also an allusion to the Venus-Mercury mystery, so significant for the chymical viewpoint. Through Christ we glimpse the union of Venus and Mercury in the 'hermaphrodite' (which for the alchymists was the 'philosopher's stone'). This union of Mercury and Venus in the 'hermaphrodite' reveals, now raised to the stage of the Mystery of the Christ-'I', the *virginal mystery of the material world*.

* * *

This contemplation has led us to distant apocalyptical, future prospects, to mysteries of renewal, enhancement, change and transfiguration also of the material world in the light and through the power of the Christ-'I', a metamorphosis of which today only a few have an idea, but which a few personalities gifted with clairvoyance already in past ages sensed as something directly perceived as in a vision. To the sensory eyes the 'star of the deep' is still hidden today in humanity's chaotic earthly night and darkness: 'Night lies in the depths.'

But we also know from our contemplations that precisely at this point when the earthly 'is come into chaos', the future with its rebirth of stars will enter, that earthly chaos and star-forces are mutually arranged, and that out of the linking of chaos and the stars a new world will be conceived. The Earth still appears to us like a grave. But precisely over graves the mystery of the eternal stars shines hopeful for the future, promising resurrection and renewal of earthly existence.

> The stars on high are silent still;
> Silent the graves, nor make reply.

In the sign (♒) that already points to a near earthly future, the Saturn characteristics of the earthly depths with the bright star-revelation of Uranus are united. In this union lies the mystery of the new alchymy. And we cannot close this whole contemplation more worthily than in that hopeful view of the future of humanity, as it has found such a revealing expression in verses 2-6 of a Freemason poem by Goethe [1749-1832]:[72]

Symbolum

HOW typical the Mason's ways
Of human life through changeful days!
Therein an analogue appears
Of his persistence, while the years
Speed on to that eternal state
Forewritten in our mortal fate.

A misty sea, the Future hides
Of joy and woe the changeful tides;
But we will press straightforward still,
To meet its thronging good and ill;
By all unswerved, undaunted, so
We to our goal may forward go.

And just before, in silent gloom,
Stands the veiled portal of the tomb;
For high and low it doth await—
The end of human pomp and state:
Where'er we pause, or onward fare,
We know our march is ended there.

In vain we ask, with yearning fond,
The form of that which lies beyond:
Interrogate them, as we will,
The stars on high are silent still;
Silent the graves, nor make reply
The dearest lips therein that lie.

While thou dost stand, with eager gaze,
Come deep foreboding and amaze;
Illusive and phantasmal forms
Disturb thy bosom with alarms:
By doubts and strange misgivings vexed,
Even the bravest are perplexed.

But hear, O Comrade! and rejoice,
The Poet's and the Sage's voice!
From all the world, and from all time,
Come their high messages sublime:
Choose well; your choice, though brief it be.
Is endless as Eternity.

Majestic Eyes do you regard,
And keep perpetual watch and ward:

Therefore, brave heart, on Heaven rely;
His fullness waits to satisfy:
The Good that Is, your faith shall share;
Work, love, and hope, and ne'er despair.

Appendix

To Chapter I:

On 'the mystery of gold' the following remarkable sentences can be found in a lecture by Rudolf Steiner, Dornach 25 Nov 1917 [GA 178]: 'For gold, the representative of the sun-like qualities within the earth's crust, does in fact enshrine an important secret. Gold stands materially in the same relationship to other substances as in the realm of thinking the concept of God does indeed to other concepts. The only question is what is made of this mystery.'

In his here frequently mentioned book *Geschichte der Alchemie* (346f.), which otherwise is valuable, Karl Christof Schmieder makes an unfortunate judgement on the Rosicrucians who are mentioned in this section that does not correspond to the facts. The author, who is well-informed on the outer history of alchemy and well-gifted with a good sense for facts, has no relationship to the esoteric, spiritual background of the realm about which he writes; he has no access for many things in this regard that are opened up to us today. His unjust judgement concerns, amongst others, Agrippa of Nettesheim (263), and Theophrastus Paracelsus (265). Concerning the latter as an alchymist, see Emil Bock, *Vorboten des Geistes*. Stuttgart: Urachhaus, 7ff.

The extract quoted in the text from Steiner's explanation of the seventh of the apocalyptic seals, 'they too are documents of genuine Rosicrucianism', runs as follows:

> Seal 7 is a representation of the 'Mystery of the Holy Grail'. It is that astral experience that gives the universal meaning of human development. The cube presents the 'spatial world', that is not yet filled by physical beings and physical characteristics. For spiritual science space is not merely 'empty', but is the carrier which in an invisible manner contains in itself all the seeds of everything physical. Out of it the whole physical is as it were precipitated, as a salt is precipitated out of the still translucent solution. And what—in relation to human beings— is formed out of the spatial world goes through the development from the lower to the higher stages. Out of the 'three dimensions of space', which are expressed in the cube, there grow first the lower human forces, made visible through the two snakes which out of themselves give birth to the purified higher nature presented in the cosmic spirals.

Through this growing upwards of these higher forces the human being can become a receptor (chalice) to receive the purely spiritual cosmic being, expressed through the dove. Through this the human being governs the spiritual, cosmic powers pictured in the rainbow. This quite sketchy description of the seal carries immeasurable depths; these can be revealed to the one who in devoted meditation allows it to work on him.

To Chapter II:

Things worth noting on 'chemistry and chymistry' are also contained in the *Fragmente des Novalis* [Fragments of Novalis], so important for all spiritual-scientific knowledge. (What follows is translated from the edition of Ernst Kamnitzer, Wolfgan Jeß Verlag, Dresden). Important individual examples:

718 ... With the specific space, there also arises the specific time and specific matter, the body ... *materia prima* is the point.

499 [important for the concept of 'chemical ether'] as for the 'sound-ether': ... chemical acoustic.

831 The chymical principle—the idea of chymistry—the materials of chymistry ... the ensouling principle, through which chymistry becomes art *a priori* I have to add.

833 At the end there also exists in chymistry no actual generically (in leaps) different matter ...

835 ... Fire is only a helper, a wise means of the chymist.

844 [interesting, to what has been mentioned from the Agriculture Course:] oxygen: the basis of the mineral realm; hydrogen: the basis of the realm of metals; carbon: the basis of vegetation; nitrogen: the basis of the animals.

There might arise possibly four chymistries, two chymical philosophies. The one proceeding from nitrogen to oxygen, the other in the opposite direction. For the one, Nature would be an unendingly modified product of oxygen ; for the other an unendingly modified nitrogen.

854 The Earth and preferably the precious stones are the most burnt bodies? Consequently, so akin to water ...

866 [Important to what was said of the relationship of the watery element to the mercurial element] ... *water consequently is a liquid metal*

chalice ... sulphur is possibly oil ... should the etheric oils be the soul of the plants? ...

[Boehme often indicated that when the 'dark' driving force, the First Principle, passes through the narrow gate of Being it divides into 'sweet water' and 'oil'. The first represents a certain harmony (Boehme calls it the 'Temperatur'); the second a warm life-force that induces still further growth and energy — *Ed.*]

To Chapter III:
On the theme '*Chaos* and *Astra*' regarding the mysteries of the process of fructification, a passage from the above-mentioned Dornach lecture (25 Nov. 1917. GA 178) is important through the manner it brings these things together with the 'mystery of gold':

> The egg does not grow out of the hen; the hen is merely the substratum for it. The growth-forces work from out of the cosmos on to the soil that has been prepared in the hen for engendering the egg. The biologist today believes that the relevant forces are all to be found within the field of his microscope. Actually, what he sees there depends on the forces of the stars which work together in a certain pattern at a given point. When we discover the cosmic at this point, then for the first time we shall have discovered the reality and the truth: it is the universe which conjures up the egg in the hen. All this is connected especially with the secret of the Sun, and in earthly terms with the secret of gold.

To Chapter IV:
To what was said on the relationship of 'Aphrodite born of the sea' to the chymical principles of *sol – mercur – sulfur*, the indication by Schmieder (*op. cit.* 359) does not appear uninteresting, but what he himself finds questionable and unbelievable, is that an alchymist, Jean Saigner, has prepared the tincture from *sea salt* in white and red.

To Chapter 5:
The realm of alchymie claimed by the alchymists for the evangelist John is mentioned in Schmieder's book in a somewhat mocking tone. But the fact he mentions that John had to work for some years in a mine on Patmos is ultimately, if taken symbolically in pictures, quite remarkable. The relationship of Novalis, so connected to the Johannine chymical spirit, to the mining profession and the chymically so important mining chapter in *Ofterdingen* comes again to mind. The legend, mentioned by Schmieder in the same connection, whereby the evangelist supposedly transformed branches into gold and pebbles

into precious stones appears as a quite important witness how in earlier times people felt the spiritual alchymy in the Johannine documents.

Also a saying of *Luther*, mentioned by Schmieder, may be mentioned here:

> The art of alchymy is justly and truly the philosophy of the ancient wise ones with which I approve, not merely because of its virtues and use in many ways, but also because of the splendid, beautiful parable it shows with the resurrection of the dead at the Last Judgement. For in the same way as the fire pulls the best out of matter and separates it from the bad, consequently leading the spirit out of the body towards the heights, that it [the spirit] possesses the better position, but matter like a dead body in which there is no longer a soul remains lying on the ground: in this way God, too, will on the Last Day through his Judgement, as through the fire, separate the just and pious from the unjust and godless. The just will be taken to heaven and live, but the unjust will be taken down to hell where they will forever remain dead.

To the Fig. of the twelve apocalyptic jewels:

It is uncertain that the ancient Greek names of the stones correspond throughout to the names today. For 'jacinth', ruby is suggested as the red precious stone. Similarly, for 'Sard' (♀ in Libra) perhaps rather the (opaque blue) turquoise; but the dictionary does not mention such a meaning for the Greek *sardion*.

The line ♒ – ♌ especially emphasizes the cosmic central axis. More on these connections in the author's book on John's Gospel, especially in the chapter on Cana (199ff.).

For the comparison of the apocalyptic earthly process and the 'alchymical process' it is important how the result of the earthly purification and earthly transformation, the New Jerusalem, carries in itself the *mystery of the gold* (Rev. 21:18; 21:21). With the apocalyptic process of metamorphosis, too, the 'pure river of gold' stands at the end. The 'mystery of gold and precious stones' already mentioned in Paradise (Gen. 2) appears on a higher level in the New Jerusalem. The white light of the paradisal carbon diamond still plays undefined in many colours. Now these colours are as it were individualized in the 'twelve apocalyptic precious stones' (of which seven are already developed into the transparently bright colours of the rainbow series). And the gold in Paradise, still connected to the ether-stream (Gen. 2:11) now appears on a higher level in connection with the 'light-filled resurrection-Earth' with the 'foundations and walls' of the Eternal City.

Key to the Signs

♈ Aries, the Ram

♉ Taurus, the Bull

♊ Gemini, the Twins

♋ Cancer, the Crab

♌ Leo, the Lion

♍ Virgo, the Virgin

♎ Libra, the Scales

♏ Scorpio, the Scorpion

♐ Sagittarius, the Archer

♑ Capricorn, the Goat

♒ Aquarius, the Waterman

♓ Pisces, the Fishes

♄ Saturn

♃ Jupiter

♂ Mars

☉ Sun

☽ Moon

☿ Mercury

♀ Venus

♅ Uranus

♁ Sulphur

⊕ Sal (Salt).

The sign for salt is usually given in the form ⊖ or θ. Yet in his book Oetinger, para. 39, emphasizes that the 'mystery of salt' is contained in the *cross*, and is only fully expressed through this figure.

♁ is the sign for the Earth, and in alchemy it also signifies antimony.

♀ is the sign for the 'philosopher's stone'. The significant placing of these two signs opposite each other, already contained in the *Rosenkreutzer-Figuren* recalls the saying of Angelus Silesius.

The Twelve Apocalyptic Jewels
(Rev. 21:19, 20)
in their relationship to the heavenly signs and planets,
with the rainbow-scale
of the seven transparent stones.

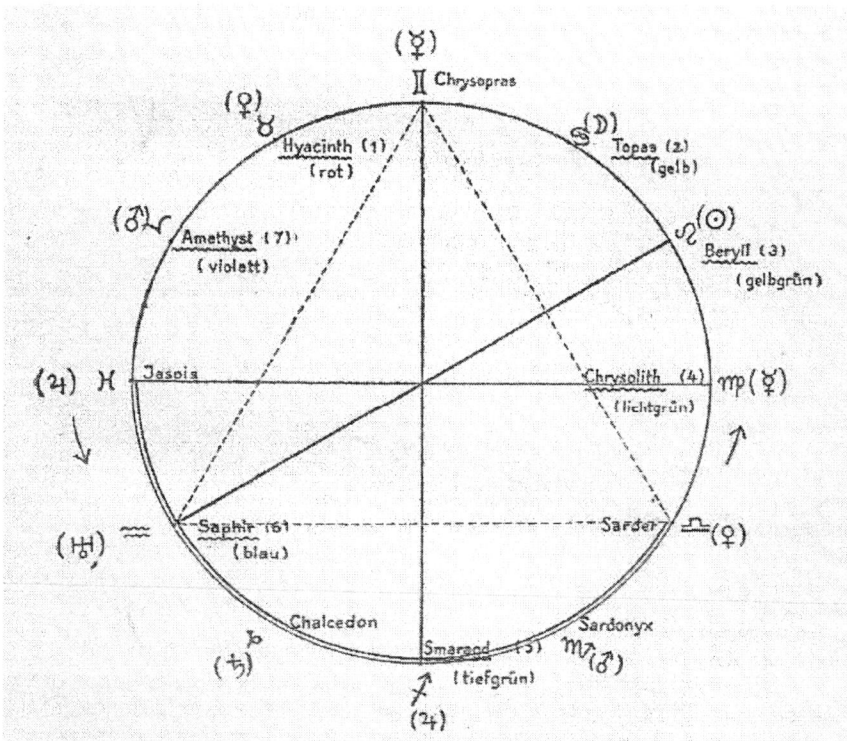

Diagram labels (reading around the circle):

(☿) ♊ Chrysopras

(♀) ♉ — Hyacinth (1) (rot)

(☽) ♋ — Topas (2) (gelb)

(♂) ♌ — Amethyst (7) (violett)

(☉) ♌ — Beryll (3) (gelbgrün)

(♃) ♓ — Jaspis

♍ (☿) — Chrysolith (4) (lichtgrün)

(♅) ♒ — Saphir (6) (blau)

♎ (♀) — Sarder

Chalcedon

(♄) ♑

Smaragd (5) (tiefgrün)

♏ (♂) — Sardonyx

(♃) ♐

Ram — amethyst
Bull — jacinth
Twins — chrysoprase
Crab — topaz
Lion — beryl
Virgin — chrysolite
Scales — agate
Scorpion — onyx
Archer — emerald
Goat — carnelian
Waterman — sapphire
Fishes — jasper

The New Jerusalem

Translator's Introduction

'Beckh agreed to write an article on the *"heavenly Jerusalem"*. To our surprise, his contribution took the form of a poem. Beckh's enthusiasm had broken the simple, elementary track; he could not make his contribution other than in an artistically lilting, poetic form. And with this unfortunately little-known poem, he shows his homeland is the spiritual world of Novalis.'

(Rudolf Frieling, 1937).

This poetic offering of Hermann Beckh's surprised his six colleagues who collaborated for the little volume on the Apocalypse, *Gegenwartsrätsel im Offenbarungslicht* ('Present-day riddles in the light of revelation'), Stuttgart 1925, pp.105–121, in the popular series *Christus aller Erde*. Based on passages from the vision of John on Patmos which we know as the Apocalypse (Book of Revelation) concluding the New Testament, Beckh's poetic lines may possibly owe something to passages from Victor Hugo's (1802–85) gigantic dream-vision *La Légende des Siècles* (1859–83) ('The legend of the ages', also tr. as 'The legend of the centuries'). Beckh himself particularly acknowledges the holistic visions and thoughts of the spiritual-scientific fragments of the early German Romantic poet and philosopher Novalis (1772–1801). Partly bursting the constraints of neat prose, Beckh, following the lead of this poetic soul with whom he felt at home, conveys an elemental vision of some essentials on the human struggle in the light of progressive Christianity.

For the task of writing on the concluding vision of the Bible — the picture of the fulfilment of the Earth — the writer no doubt felt he had to risk everything for this ultimate theme by attempting a poetic mode. Like a sketch-book, a workshop, or an 'improvisation', in facing pictures from the Apocalypse existential demands will inevitably use whatever lends itself as relevant to the high spiritual theme — Beckh's own love of the mountains, traditional pictures, fairy-tales, the Christian liturgy, Wagner's *Parsifal* and the Grail story, alchemical and spiritual-scientific insights—above all following the poet and miner Novalis, as pathfinder to express the unity of star and stone, of man and the world, the self and its Creator.

A spiritual experience as a five-year-old in the mountains convincing him of human pre-existence was decisive for Beckh's life. Something of the incredible pain of compassion for his fellow man he experienced is also reflected in this poetic offering (see Beckh's autobiographical memoirs in the biography by Gundhild Kačer-Bock, *Hermann Beckh Leben und Werk*, Stuttgart 1997, p. 70; Eng. tr. Anastasi 2016).

This rendering into English, making no poetic claims, hopes nevertheless to remain faithful to the author's text—(A. S., 2014).

The New Jerusalem

Hermann Beckh

A clear winter's day enticed me
into the solitude of the high mountains. Today the mountains are
not only the great grave, not just a heap of rubble
of the Earth, of the lonely dying one
that longs to disappear again into world dust.
Today they are a mirror of the eternal Light,
which shone in the primal beginning, of the virginal
crystal formative forces that are reveal in rock crystals
and in the tender miraculous starry snowflakes
the pure cosmic light.
Today everything earthly is covered
with a radiant dress of heavenly light,
from myriads of tiny snow-crystals
a shining countenance of the Sun glitters towards me
and reflects the heavens,
in that which, falling out of the heights of heaven
has then become the tender earthly covering.

Only out there, where on the far horizon
the widths of the flat-land broaden before the eye
and where in the nebulous grey fog begin to disappear
the towns of the people, heavy darkness weighs,
dark stripes of blue-black billowing fog.
    Is it the pressure
of demonic shadows on human souls?
    Does there not shine
to them also the brightness of eternal Light?

Does it not penetrate to their dark sheaths yet?
'The cosmic Light shone into the darkness' —
thus it is written — 'and the darkness
comprehended it not.' But up here,
here in the freedom of the mountains,
in the pure light, the clear cosmic-'I' shines pure;
here speaks in the profound blue ether of the sky
out of the widths of the world the sublime primal mystery
of the Darkness, which yet did comprehend the Light.
And from the foothills of the Alps, which the winter
bequeathed with the bright, radiant dress,
where spring flowers are already promisingly
blossoming at the edge of the snow, now in mid-winter,
the gaze is lifted towards those scented, distant snowy mountains
which yet in the clear light of the winter's day
glisten there in eternal white as if within reach.
As if condensed out of the ether-light of the clouds,
like a revelation of supersensory beings,
like the shining Temple of the distant Grail,
thus it stands before the astonished gaze,
like that mysterious town of Arcturus,
the town of the ice-flowers and the crystal-plants
beheld by the fairytale eye of Novalis.
And in the soul's divining dawning
the picture of the Holy City condenses,
which with golden walls transparent like crystal
with gates pearl-like for the spirit-eye
of the seer on the holy island of the sea
showed itself in the loneliness of his soul,
and which in the coloured light of the gemstones
reveal twelvefold sublime cosmic-forces of stones
and cosmic-forces of stars:

'And behold! He led me in the spirit
on to a high and sublime mountain
and showed me the holy city Jerusalem,
descending from the world above
of pure heavenly light and radiating
in the splendour of revelation of the divine world.
And I, John, saw the holy city
like a virgin who, in a white dress
adorned like a bride, prepares herself for the wedding.'
A festive moment of existence, well do I feel it,

is the one which conjures this shining picture of revelation
for me before the eye of my soul,
one of the moments when the veils,
which otherwise cover up the spiritual before the sensory gaze,
seem to lift lightly, only a little,
and where the 'I' can feel itself again
'weaving in widths of space and depths of time':
and where it is again connected to the cosmic light,
and in this cosmic light with everything which otherwise
radiates to it in the mirror of the outer world,
where it begins to divine again:
the force which there weaving in the ether-light
of the snow-crystals enchants constellations of stars,
and which out of this in the soft spume of the flakes
condenses winter's white earthly cover,
the force, which then from that which in our being
has been hardened, fashions the mountain crystal,
which in the heavy stone the counter-pole of weight:
wants to reveal light, this force
am I . . . I am this too,
who, to this world, which today in the light of the heights
radiates towards me, has given death—
to the world which as the valley of the shadow of death
appeared often to me, is at other times
as a great grave of dust and rubble . . .
the rocky grave where Moses with his exalted power
was laid to sleep by the Father-God,
afterwards, on the holy mountain height once more,
for the last time in his life there shone for him
the eternal Light of the divine I AM,
after he had heard once more in the Light
the eternal primal Word, which once revealed Itself
to him tremendously by speaking:
'I am I, Who was and is and will be.'

The power of the gods, which once created the universe
and entered into the human 'I', has
separated this human 'I' from the universe.
Thereby this universe has died,
has become a grave for what lives.
In one lightning flash of sudden understanding
the obscure words of Novalis light up:
'Whether perhaps Nature has been turned

to stone by the gaze of God? —
or for sheer terror at the advent of man? . . .'

For the power of the gods creates in the primal beginning
the human divine 'I' in the Spirit-light;
through the power of the Earth the earthly 'I' grew in him
and only in the becoming of this earthly 'I'
the power in earthly matter became dead stone.
The human 'I' which created this death
also possesses the power to transform it,
since Christ has connected Himself with the Earth.
Only in Him do I find my true 'I'
that is raised above all powerlessness
into which the sickness of sin has banished it.
And as if awakening to myself in musing,
I recognize in the resting thought:
Yea! Also in yourself, in the depth of your soul,
there slumbers the germinating-power of the eternal 'I',
which like a grain of corn has been sown
into everything that dies in earthly being.
Christ has planted it there. Also in you
it rests buried, also in you it awaits
the resurrection. Only if you too
burst in yourself the dark husk of the grave,
you can become a co-creator in creations of soul
working at Earth's transformation,
at its resurrection, which the Earth then
experiences in a new and transfigured being,
when what of the old Earth is dying
will one day have fallen into dust and ashes,
so that the living, the new Earth
can spring forth out of that which as ash
of the living is dispersed in the universe.
And again I hear a profound saying of Novalis
within my soul, when he speaks of the One,
'Who moved solely by love for us
gave Himself completely for us, and into the Earth,
laid Himself as a Foundation-Stone of a divine City.'
In the Mystery, which in this word
he speaks to us, a veil is lifted
off the secret which John beheld,
when from the high mountain he saw
(which spirit-led he had climbed in spirit)

the divine Holy City, Jerusalem,
in its bridal, virginal adornment.

There, that city of our human present-day,
the large city that on the far horizon
in the dusty haze hides from the eye,
the city which once delighted the heart of the child,
when I, a stranger, entered it for the first time
in early youth, which still today
awakens in the heart joyful memories,
she too is built up out of what has died,
out of dead Earth's rigid, stony matter,
and what moves in it carries the seed of death.
One day the following word will become truth for it, too:
'Woe! she is fallen, the great city!'
Into the earthly grave there returns what arose from it.
Yet that holy city of the future of the Earth,
which John's seer eyes beheld,
did not arise out of the dark earthly ground,
she is not from below; she is from above,
from the realm of the incorruptible, of the ether-light.
As in the snow-crystal's ether-spume
a bright cosmic starry life
is condensed to a tender veil of earthly matter,
as all earthly matter has this starry life
as its being's true origin,
thus in that bright city the life
but returns to its starry origin,
no longer polluted by decay
which in enchantment held it here below.

The human 'I' which created the enchantment
in stone and plant as in its own being,
alone has the power to free the fetters
when, having gone through the cleansing of many lives
and trials of suffering,
it re-unites with the star-borne 'I'
which descended to Earth in Christ.
With starry ether-light earthly matter
will then be shone through again.
And this earthly material flooded by heavenly light
will become the new Earth, germinating,
which will only know development, growth and unfolding,
but no longer any decay.

It is the Earth, which the one consecrated by God,
illuminated by Christ's light, was allowed to behold
in the pure revelation of cosmic light,
about which he spoke the transfigured words:
'And I beheld a new heaven
and a new earth': for the first heaven
(which as the upper world of the radiating light
separated itself from the weaving of earthly matter
in the primal beginning of creation) has passed away,
with it the Earth, as it was before,
and also the sea — no more to be seen.
Then the voice from the throne becomes true:
'Now the dwelling of God is with men,
and He, the Holy One, will live with them.
They will be His faithful people,
and as their divine "I" He will live with them.
Death will be overcome, and every tear
God Himself will wipe from their eyes.'
'Behold I make all things new' — in these words
is enclosed the Mystery of *transformation*:
already when on Golgotha the Christ
burst victoriously the dark covering of the grave,
when His corpse dissolved and disappeared,
and when in light-transfigured corporeality
the disciples then beheld the Risen One,
then the transformation of the Earth had begun
which shall continue into future cycles of time.
Since then the Holy City is unfolding,
although still hidden to earthly senses,
but the deeper sensing of the heart beholds
it everywhere already in the present
where human beings in shared faithful work
build a place for spiritual life,
and where the purest sacrificial forces of the heart
unite with the sense for noble form.
Everything outer may appear as dead,
may even be fallen and rotten,
yet there rises still visible to the finer senses,
out of what is dying, in a tender outline
the bright beautiful picture of the becoming.
Like from everything we humans carry
in ourselves as dead, as the decay of spirit,
stench spreads everywhere,

thus also from everything that in ourselves
our 'I' has shone through and enlivened,
life's creative breath penetrates into everything earthly.
And nothing of all this that in this way
the human being has wrestled from his own being,
remains lost for the Earth's future.
What he thinks in the spirit, feels in the heart,
what in deeds he reveals through his will,
what in doing he embodies into matter,
what his whole being expresses,
it carries the seed of the new earth in itself.
And though in these earthly days he still
feels distant from such soul-creating,
in soul-*depths* it has already begun.
In the heart the Foundation Stone has been laid
upon which one day the city shall be founded,
which shines in uncorrupted nature,
a shining Temple of divine, eternal being.
Within, as a living pillar there lives
the human being who overcame the past,
and who received the name 'I' from God
(around which the eternal name Eve
is wound as a Mystery of the virgin bride).
And it is only the nightmare of decay
(the Sphinx which did not yet plunge into the abyss)
which today still hides this from the senses.

And like awakening from a dream of the distant future
my eye turns towards the horizon,
to that sombre blue layer of fog,
which distantly covers the widths of the flatland
like that dismal and dark realm of shadows
of the Fates in Novalis' fairytale world,
who forever spin further the old [patterns]
and towards that which stirs eternally youthful,
setting itself childlike creatively into existence
they contemplate ruin — in vain — in poisonous hate.
In the fog I behold the nightmare of decay,
as it bears Sphinx-like on the earthly souls.
From the beings who dwell down there,
it hides the world of light in the heights
into which destiny full of grace has allowed me
to look from this mountain today.

I feel indeed: until the foggy, Sphinx-like
dark, demonic pressure in human souls
is not expelled by the clear light of the 'I'
as long as decay reigns Medusa-like
in soul-darkness and soul-dullness,
in drives and passions,
as long as it is not overcome there,
until then the 'I' cannot be master
in its outer husks,
until then earthly matter remains enchanted,
and in the soul there only remains the light-filled divining
of the distant divine city.
Transformation has to begin within
before it can be revealed full of light
one day in outer earthly being.
There where the fog weighs down in the depths,
down there you too have to continue dwelling
working among your human brothers
until all the nightmare darkness is overcome,
and only the memory of what you have beheld here,
what was experienced in the pure light of the heights,
you take with you as a comfort into those depths.
While I was thus lost in thought,
see there, all at once,
the fog of memories' weaving pictures is seized.
Before my soul lives another picture
(this too I experienced wandering in the mountains) —
there the fog does not remain in the blue of the widths,
darkening it penetrated into the mountains,
breathlessly chased by the wild wind's bride,
who whipped them into shreds.
The foggy shreds' chaotic, fantastic forms,
they became demonic figures
and before the inner gaze of the soul
there appeared the wild chase of the Apocalyptic riders
with pale reddish sulphuric armour,
with horses whose heads, lion-like,
blow sulphurous billows out of their nostrils
and whose tails are made of snake-heads,
and they have power over mankind.
Ghostlike everything lives in them
that holds the soul in the fog of greed,
resisting the higher 'I'.

They are the powers that rule in the fog,
which put the nightmare on to human souls
robbing them of the view of heavenly light,
and give them over to death's power of decay.
And in the soul itself there reigns decay.
Here first it must be overcome,
erroneous drives have to be transformed,
which have estranged themselves from starry life
where lies their beings' purer source.
Only then can starry life shine again
in the rigid stone which today still surrounds the grave
in which the human 'I' is bound.
Only then the earthly body is also able
to tear itself away from the power of decay;
the Earth itself can unite with Heaven
(as it separated from heaven once
in the primal beginnings of creation ...).

The purifying transformation
which worked in purity of thought, light-filled,
drawing the human soul from the powers of decay,
it has its outer counter-picture
in that which working in the earthly realm of matter
works against rot and decay,
in the *salt*, which, condensing out of solution,
builds forms that meaningfully, sublime,
in earthly being can reveal to the spiritual gaze
the secrets of the spatial world
where the primal crystal form becomes the temple-form,
the cube as long as wide, as wide as high.
Thus the eternal measure of spatial forming
carries as formative force within itself the human 'I',
which overcame the fog of decay
(still it hangs on coarser sheaths,
which then the soul discards as
the 'forecourt, given to the heathens').
And this measure the human being also carries
into the city where no temple shines
for then the divine Light shining in him
is the temple itself, because then everything
has become a single temple and all life
has become sacred temple service.

From these future pictures I am led away

by memory to a past year,
where I found myself in a fairytale world
of wonderful snow and ice crystals.
But unlike the outer world as it was today —
which shone in fresh green of May,
and burst with the spring's flowery adorning.
Only within was the world of snow and ice.
And in this world of snow and ice crystals
a familiar fairytale picture was created for me,
the picture of a child which as white as snow
as red as blood, as black as ebony wood,
on a high mountain in a crystal coffin
lay in a sleep of death,
wept over by friendly animals showing pity,
owl and raven, nocturnal birds,
fluttered around; the dove lightly hovered above;
the child, who suffering, lovingly sacrificed itself
to the darkness, which spinning the threads of envy
planned evil to it, but only sleep of death
could bring, that could not cloud
its pure being with the poison of selfishness.
Thus in death it appeared sleeping —
the radiant colour of life,
life's blossoming colour remains,
the fresh red of its cheeks, because the decay
could not reach its bright being.
There it lay in its coffin of crystal,
until it awoke at the green bush
(it was a sprouting sapling of the miraculous tree,
the Tree of Life growing in Paradise).
The young sovereign power of the cosmic 'I'
could waken it there to full life
making *Snow-White* Queen of the World
kissed awake by the cosmic starry love.

The profound secret of the *Holy Grail*
I recognize in the simple fairytale scene:
the sufferings of Christ and the Resurrection
of the flesh which is the coffin of the Spirit.
That which on Earth resists decay,
the pure strength of the stone which in the crystal
is revealed as power of cosmic light,
becomes the coffin of the body of the pure child

Karl Thylmann, 'Snow-White' (woodcut 30 × 32 cm), 1914.

that overcame the sickness of decay,
which became healthy again as a starry being
where the stone's crystal purity lives,
but the stone's weight is overcome.
This substance of life that has become a crystal coffin
penetrated by ether-light
that is removed from the power of decay
it is the *Holy Grail.*
In the crystalline becoming of the etheric,
there time, which serves decay,
becomes again space. This is the secret of the Grail.
Time which in the world of decay
is the destroyer of being for man:
for man, who will-less experiences becoming and decay,
time is governed by the awakening 'I',
which takes becoming and dying into the will
which then will-less experiences eternity in both.
And through eternity transformed
time becomes space. That etheric being,
which is only experienced in the becoming of time,
(in the same way as the plant wants to reveal its etheric being
in the germinating, growing, flowering, bearing fruit
as a being of time),

it then becomes penetrated by the essence of space,
which in a crystalline, spatial form is imprinted.
In this transformation works the power of the Grail.

The same elevated secret of starry light
that is sealed in the realm of stones,
is beheld by the seer in the most sublime picture:
in the soul's separateness, the Leader showed him
on holy Patmos, in the picture of the Holy City Jerusalem,
which to him had descended out of cosmic light,
appearing in revelatory splendour,
like a bride adorned for her wedding.
Where time becomes space, where ether-beings
mysteriously wed to the earthly world,
and where in the light of the spirit this is beheld,
transfigured earthly-heavenly being appears
in the full circle of twelvefold ether-colours,
(so too the pure ether time-being
speaks in the sevenfold bow of colour).
'Is there anyone who already understood the Mystery
of the stones and the stars,' so speaks Novalis,
'I cannot say I know, but certainly
he must have been a sublime being.'
To the one who spoke this and he who has given to us
the Revelation, this Mystery was known.
The 'I', which has become the lord in the forces of space,
can in the body, the un-decaying one,
then unfold a twelvefold starry life,
which in the gemstones' twelvefold coloured light
is revealed reflecting twelvefold on earth.
This twelvefold stellar life which in stones
is reflected twelvefold the seer saw
in the bright ground of that divine city,
and that twelvefold exalted cosmic power,
which out of the twelve starry signs radiates to us,
there builds up the new human body,
which is un-decaying like a gemstone,
which again is a temple divine.
Once, in distant pre-earthly Paradise,
there the human body was etheric-divine,
was the green garden still in the land of Eden,
was also the Ark, which life-saving,
swam then on the wild waves of the Deluge.

In the temple then it found its exalted symbol,
which Solomon created through Hiram's art.
In Jesus it became the pure human Body,
which in the bright divine City of Earth's future
is transformed again into the cosmic Temple
and out of the pure being of the crystals,
in which weave the cosmic forces of the Twelvehood,
there sprouts a new, bright Tree of Life,
which unites ether-force of time with the force of space,
that brings healing to all human beings
through the healing balsamic force of its leaves.
It is watered by the eternal stream of life,
the sacred fourfold stream of Paradise,
that is sealed in the world cross,
the source which quickens all those who thirst
at the Supper of the Lamb and the Bride
(which is the living New Earth).
In its blossoming and fruit-bearing
the same starry Twelve is revealed.
It gives its fruit each month.
The order of space is imprinted into the course of time,
When space and time are transformed through eternity.

I had lost myself in distant contemplation.
The Sun of this short winter day sinks,
and cold darkness descends on the mountains.
The world of the light of the heights has disappeared,
sunk down is the splendour of its revelation.
The world again is a wide grave.
Yet in the heights the stars still quietly shine;
the brightest is the Star of Christmas.
And what was beheld in the light of the heights
continues to live as warmth thankfully in the heart,
as comfort in life and hope for the future.
And even if my path still leads over graves,
and I have still to carry death,
yet there shines on the path from cosmic distances
the holy solemn light of the silent stars.

Snow-white

('*Schneewittchen*', in *Die Christengemeinschaft*, 1. Jg. 5, Aug. 1924, pp. 138–146.)

The soul of our ancient forefathers listened deep into the mysteries of the events of nature, of the blossoming and decaying of the plant world, of their dying and annual rejuvenation. They perceived the language of the spirit in the whispering and rustling of the tree-tops in the forest, in everything which was revealed in the changing pictures of the seasonal cycle of the year. Through the manner of its feelings for nature the Teutonic soul became especially deeply receptive for the revelation of Christianity, for the great mystery of death and resurrection. That which existed in the ancient natural feeling in the pre-divining Christian understanding was fostered in the early Mysteries as conscious knowledge of the spirit. This, linked later with true Christian content, lived on in the magic of the German fairy-tales.

* * *

Let us place ourselves spiritually into that part of deep winter in which we live towards the time of the deepest darkness of the year that brings us again the ascent to the light. The religiously attuned soul open to the spirit in world-events can experience quite directly this time of the year, as if out of the widths of space full of grace something in truth wants to descend to the Earth. As if from the spiritual light, cosmic light and cosmic love want to bless and warm us.

In the rigidity of natural life, in the outer darkness of the year, the Earth as a spiritual being is most awake. The soul of the Earth receives the Spirit, which from the realms of the stars comes down to her. Why are we filled with such joy on seeing the snowflakes falling at that time? Does the soul unconsciously feel how from the heights of the light, full of grace, something trickles and streams down to the Earth? And the mysterious star-formations of the snowflake-ice-crystals — are they not like crystals of light? Like a cosmic starry life that before our eyes is as it were consolidated into that tender bright virginal veil of the element of earth? Do we not find in the essence of snow the great mystery of the original weaving of all earthly matter made out of cosmic light?

Everything earthly is crystallised and condensed out of etheric light. This is revealed in the snow.

In all their outer coldness something like spiritual warmth, like warming love, emanates from silently falling flakes, from the maternal covering of snow, which so softly and lovingly covers the rigid Earth protecting the shoots slumbering in the depths. The maternal element of the world speaks to us out of this warming love. And out of our own soul it speaks, if the soul has learnt not only to be with itself, but to look up to that which it still carries as a seed in itself. It looks up to that being that wants to become when the soul has learned to die, to sacrifice itself for this spirit-child who is coming about. 'In each of us,' says Novalis, 'there lives the heavenly Mother in order to give birth eternally to every child.'[73] In that which wants to become the higher 'I' is at work, connecting again to the cosmic light and opening to the cosmic love.

The Act of Consecration of Man of The Christian Community should help us to awaken in our soul that mood of offering of self-sacrifice, to that in us which spiritually wants to become truly human. In looking up to this higher picture of the human being we speak the words over what is being offered, 'Receive it from our pure thinking, our loving heart, our willing devotion'. The whole trinity of our inner being is to be purified and penetrated with light by the divine. The forces of crystal-clear purity then live in our thinking, the forces of warm love in our feelings, and the forces of highest devotion, noblest mood of offering in our will. And looking around in the sensory world, this purity of thinking then shines to us again in the colour of the white snow. Warmth of love lives for us in the red blood. With the red drops of blood that fall on the snow, a loving earthly element is added to the pure light of the heights that shines in the white snow. In Wolfram von Eschenbach's *Parzifal* the young hero's pure virginal love is presented to his spiritual eye in this picture. Our forces of will and willing devotion there spring from the dark depths of the 'I' that dwells in the holy-of-holies of the soul, of which the outer picture for us is the black colour of midnight, or of the burnt wood. What we called before our soul of the essence of the snow that originates in the light of the heights, lives again spiritually with the two other soul-colours in that child which the fairy-tale calls *Schneewittchen*, Snow-white.

The beginning of the fairy-tale of Snow-white conjures up the mood of Advent for us. Expectation of the Spirit wanting to connect with the Earth is what we as it were behold in the picture of the descending snowflakes. In the ancient Mysteries it was still known how especially at this time of the year spiritual forces as well as soul-forces stream down to the Earth from cosmic heights. Mystery-centres existed where the becoming and growth of the human seed destined to become the carrier of future world-content was consciously guided in such a way that this [spiritual] seed as the Christmas-child sees the light of day. It seems that the fairy-tale of Snow-white was inspired precisely out of such Mysteries.

What we find as actual Christian content in this fairy-tale was already in existence in the depths of the early Mysteries before it became an outer earthly event on Golgotha. The fairy-tale of Snow-white places before us a Mystery in the highest and purest manner. Through the child-like element of the whole fairy-tale it gains its actual magic. It is the ancient Mystery of suffering, death and resurrection, the profound mystery of all becoming of which the cycle of the year also speaks to us with ever renewed persistence. Inwardly religious participation in the seasons can lead us deeply into the mysteries of the fairy-tale of Snow-white. In the sequence of moods of its individual sections we can find again and experience the moods of the seasons and of the religious festivals that occur in it. From the mood of Advent we are led to the mood of Christmas; from there to the mood of fasting, Passiontide, the Good-Friday mood; from there to Easter and resurrection, until the whole finds an ending in a kind of midsummer with the mood of St John's-tide.

* * *

The soul, when it is blessed with it, finds in itself the maternal being, which is prepared to die for the becoming spirit-child. The egoism of the soul is also found as a lower self; another power that wants to take the life of that child, of the being that wants to become in us, which is higher, more loving and purer than we ourselves. That power is called the stepmother in the fairy-tale. The higher maternal element is the warm, sacrificial love. The other power is that which lives as the forces in matter. Matter is connected with the primal word for 'mother', Latin *mater*. We found that higher maternal element in the warming and protecting element of the covering of snow; the outer coldness of the snow is that element that belongs to the essence of matter. We saw the condensing of the primal light, a crystalizing and consolidating of the original light-filled etheric is the whole essence of matter. Through the coldness, all this condensing and consolidating takes place, just as water freezes to ice through the coldness. In coldness, spiritually seen, there live forces of hate, in the same way as the warmth of the Sun that melts the ice into water, forces of cosmic love live. Ultimately the entire essence of matter, of the condensed earthly element, rests on the forces of hate.

The soul, too, that is given completely to the weight of the earthly element carries in itself those forces of hate, of envy, of all those feelings through which it is estranged from its higher self and the divine that wants to live in her (the soul). Separation from the divine, according to its original nature, is the earthly Fall of Man. The fairy-tale pictorially expresses the essence of that which strives towards separation when it speaks of the preparation of the poisoned apple. For this the stepmother goes 'into a solitary chamber, quite hidden away'. Already the story of Paradise, in the picture of the fruit that the tempter gives to man through Eve, presents the forces of selfishness, the ego-forces through which the human being separates himself from the divine. The 'I' should have been a gift of the gods for mankind. But this gift is double-edged, because through the power of the tempter one-sidedly turned towards the Earth, it separates the human being in selfishness from the divine. The fairy-tale expresses in the picture of the apple this double-edged nature of the earthly fruit of the 'I', whose one side is poisoned. The loving soul that allows the spirit-child in itself to come to life awakens to the higher 'I' by connecting again with the divine. The soul filled with hate and jealousy, turned towards the earthly element, is intent on the life of the spirit-child. This soul poisons the divine gift of the 'I' towards lower egoism, into selfishness, of which the divine child dies.

In the picture, too, of sunlight and moonlight we can see the essence of these two soul-qualities. In the warm sunlight live the forces of radiant love, pouring forth, giving of itself. In the cold lunar element those forces live that reflect the sunlight, mirroring it, that pull the light to themselves, wanting to keep it to themselves, who want themselves to shine and glitter in the borrowed light. We look as in a mirror into the world when we look spiritually towards these powers of the Moon. This mirroring effect lives in all the forces of the intellect in the human soul. Through this we can approach the mystery of the magic mirror, in which the evil queen looks at herself and at the earthly events. This lunar-like mirror of matter gives her true knowledge, self-knowledge, and knowledge of the surpassing qualities of others. But it is a self-seeking self-knowledge, knowledge that awakens envy and deadly hate in her heart.

However, forces of another kind, the Sun-forces of love, Sun-ego forces, live in Snow-white. Consequently, when she enters the Sun-age at seven years old she is described as 'beautiful as the clear day'. Primal childlike qualities live in the soul that is called to the Highest. And so, in the fairy-tale of Snow-white that Being, in Whom immeasurably deeply and meaningfully the great Mystery takes place, stands before us as a young innocent Child. This enchantment of the childlike is poured out over all the events that take place. The highest Mystery takes place through those Sun-'I' forces that do not recoil or retreat from the earthly situation, but who lay hold of the earthly situation, even of earthly evil and the self-seeking element, penetrating and transforming it. The highest expression for this penetration and transformation of the earthly through the powers of the Sun-being is the Mystery of Golgotha. And in Snow-white the sublime Christian Mystery finds its childlike, fairy-tale reflection.

Because it contains this confrontation with the earthly forces of evil, Snow-white's Mystery path from the beginning is a path of suffering, or sacrificial love. The apple, too, she does not take out of greed – 'Anlustern' has nothing to do with 'Lust, desire', but to look with curiosity – but because she recognized the value, even though double-edged, of the gift of the 'I', because she feels that she also has to take up these forces into herself in order to transform and overcome them. Evil remains inwardly foreign to her. Like a foreign body, the 'poisonous piece' flies out of her when the coffin touches the 'bush', the sprouting bush of life. All the pursuits and attacks of the forces of evil reigning in earthly matter can only serve this pure soul to lead her (the soul) to ever-higher degrees. Ultimately, it finds marriage with the highest 'I' living in the cosmic light, being kissed awake by cosmic love. The path of suffering becomes for her the highest initiation, the path into higher worlds.

* * *

Already the beginning of this path brings the encounter with that which lives as life-robbing forces in the world, of that which in the soul itself exists as death-bringing forces. In the Imaginative consciousness the soul experiences the forces of greed emanating from itself as wild animals that want to pounce on the soul. As such the soul runs about in the forest, whose twilight darkness the soul has to stride through before the entrance into the realms of light of the higher spiritual world. In the hunter sent by the evil step-mother, Snow-white meets the death-bringing power. But the plea of her innocent heart is stronger than the power that wants to kill. The innocent soul of Snow-white has no part in the forces of death and greed. Consequently, she is unaffected by the wild animals of the forest. They 'ran past her and did her no harm'.

We find the meeting with the hunter in many pictorial accounts of the path of the Mysteries. The forest, too, is the great borderland in many fairy-tales and legends. In the legend of Parzifal by Wolfram von Eschenbach it is the forest before the Grail Castle where Parzifal meets the Guardian of the Grail realm who demands of him the payment of death. He fights with him and gains the Grail horse that carries him to the Grail Castle — but only after further long journeys, for Parzifal is not yet mature. Many things point to an inner connection of the sources out of which the Parzifal legend and the fairy-tale of Snow-white are inspired. We already found in the drops of blood on the snow a motif of the Parzifal legend. Parzifal rides without rest from early morning till evening — 'what he rode in one day, a bird would have difficulties to fly' — until he arrives at evening at the Grail Castle. Snow-white runs over 'thorns and sharp stones ... as long as her legs would carry her' until at nightfall she finds the little cottage of the dwarves — for everything in this fairy-tale is measured child-size. This decisive progress is essentially significant for the soul that seeks the path into the spiritual world. The soul does not look to the past, to that which it has lost, but only into the future, towards that which it should become. This decision lives in the language of the fairy-tale in Snow-white's words, 'I'm willing to run into the wild forest and never come back home again.'

Descriptions of Mystery paths speak of all kinds of experiences of trials, of horrors, threshold experiences through which the soul has to go especially during the time of Advent before the significant experience of Christmas. And they speak to us of the tremendous feeling of loneliness that overcomes the soul at the threshold of the spiritual world, when it has taken its leave of everything that until now was the well-known environment for its consciousness. She has to take leave of everything that was dear to her and to which she came close; the future lies strange and unknown before her. When it first enters that transition realm before the threshold, the soul experiences as though it has to feel through every single detail of its new surroundings as though split apart, as an intimate knower of that spiritual path tells us (Rudolf Steiner, *The Road to Self-Knowledge*. GA 16). In the language of the fairy-tale, it says, 'Now the poor child was all alone in the big forest and became so frightened that she even eyed all the leaves of the trees and didn't know what to do.'

After leaving the earthly realm and passing through the transition realm to the threshold, the soul finally enters the first realm of the higher world, a realm of etheric spirituality. In the Parzifal legend, the Grail Castle appears here to us, in the child-like context of the fairy-tale Snow-white as the cottage of the dwarves. What is beheld here can no longer be measured with earthly measurements; it glows in fine, tender, etheric, super-earthly purity: 'In the cottage everything was tiny but indescribably pretty and neat.' The fairy-tale tells us quite clearly in its language that a realm of higher worlds has truly been entered. For what does it mean, 'Snow-white over the mountains'? What is the 'mountain' in the fairy-tale, and what is the mountain generally? We all know that it obscures the view into the valley beyond. We have to climb it ourselves and in so doing take away the separating wall in order to see across. When we are down in the valley, what lies beyond is invisible, on 'the other side'. In fairy-tales generally the mountain is a picture of the separating wall preventing us from looking into what is invisible to the physical senses, into the spiritual world. Through inner development and strengthening of the soul we can take away this separating wall before our soul's vision. In the Gospel this inner soul-strength that opens the spiritual eye is called 'faith'. Christ's words of the 'faith which moves mountains' receives through this a new light from a new side.

Snow-white's soul has now entered a new supersensory world beyond the physical senses, a world 'beyond the mountains', into a region of etheric spiritual beings. They are called the seven dwarves. Seven central forces reign in this etheric world, in this world of etheric light, which we find when we look out into the starry realms as the beings of the seven planets – in the earlier spiritual sense, not in today's astronomy: Sun, Moon, Mercury, Venus, Mars, Jupiter and Saturn. When we look down towards the earthly element, into the Earth's interior, we find the beings of the seven basic metals – gold, silver, copper, quicksilver, iron, tin and lead. Here, too, we should not think with the chemistry of today of the physical, mineral element, but what the awakened, finer etheric senses can experience with these physical minerals. The fairy-tale does not remain content with the general saying that all earthly material derives from the forces of etheric light, but concretely we are to recognize that the etheric-spiritual element of the individual metals relates to the etheric activity of light. They reach the Earth, radiating through specific planetary spheres. These beings of the metals are the earthly reflections of active cosmic-etheric forces.

If we look here at the spirituality reigning only around the Earth itself, we find the gnome-like elemental spiritual beings. They are the 'seven dwarves' of the fairy-tale, who in the mountains 'hack and dig for metal ore'; we think of the seven basic metals corresponding to the individual beings. This earthly spirituality is, again, a reflection of planetary spirituality that governs over it. Etheric planetary light appears in the Earth as the metals. The etheric being of the Sun appears as gold, of the Moon as silver, of Mars as iron [Mercury as quicksilver, Venus as copper, Jupiter as tin, Saturn as lead]. This sphere of etheric spirituality cannot be entered by the soul with the habitual earthly self, but can only enter with its own etheric being. The soul feels it becomes split up, divided between the seven planetary forces. But one amongst the seven spheres is there, which in a certain sense unites and gathers into itself the essence of all the others. All this expressed in the pictorial language of the fairy-tale in a childlike, charming manner which can be found by everyone for themselves. Whoever knows the traditional signs of the seven planets — which in alchemy were at the same time the signs for the corresponding basic metals — can seek and find them in the seven individual attributes that play a role in the astonished questions of the dwarves returning home ('little chair', 'little plate', and so on).

Let us look at the place in the fairy-tale where Snow-white, after she had beforehand lain in the six other beds, finally falls asleep in the seventh one. The soul first in sleep enters the higher worlds. Waking up the next morning, the wakening in that higher world would then be the next higher level. There the soul also beholds the spiritual beings of that world which she initially only enters during sleep. Only then can these spiritual beings appear, revealing themselves when all the light of the senses is completely obscured.

> When it had got quite dark, the masters of the cottage came home; they were the seven dwarves who with pick and shovel mined for ore in the mountains ... they lighted their seven little candles. ...

Only in the deepest darkness of the outer senses can the light of the spiritual world shine, the same way as in the cycle of the year the shining up of the Christmas light falls into the deepest darkness of the year. That moment when the seven dwarves with their seven candles stand around the bed of the sleeping Snow-white admiring the beauty of the child, we can feel as the high-point of the *Christmas experience in the fairy-tale*, as the flaming up of the spiritual Christmas light. The Christmas mood seems to be poured over the whole charming and most lovely episode of the fairy-tale. We can think about the experience of the soul of a child, who before the lights of the Christmas tree feels dreamily transported into a higher world, a world of etheric light.

* * *

But already the awakening in the morning brings new tasks, a sobering mood of fasting follows the mood of Christmas. The soul shall learn in the world in which it has now awakened, devotedly to serve the spiritual powers. With such intentions she approaches it. And the soul, when she really inwardly belongs to those worlds, can do no other than say 'Yes' with a whole heart to what the spiritual world demands of her. Completely pure, strong and childlike, this deep inner confirmation sounds out of the answer Snow-white gives to the dwarves when they ask her whether she will keep house for them, 'cook, make the beds, wash, sew and knit' and so on. 'Yes, gladly with all my heart,' Snow-white answers, 'and stayed with them'. In this passage speaking of the devoted serving, we can feel the mood of the Washing of the Feet of Christian initiation.

The warning of the dwarves is well founded, not to allow the wicked stepmother to enter, for into this world of etheric spirituality the forces of the lower 'I', forces of the lower self, can find entrance. Letting in these forces would bring death to the higher life. Snow-white, in her being, has nothing in common with these forces, but her path, which consequently leads her into much higher worlds than the mere etheric world of the seven dwarves, is precisely the path of confrontation with those forces of earthly matter and the earthly 'I'. In letting these forces in, she has to take them up, transform and overcome them. Through this her path certainly becomes a path of highest suffering. Snow-white suffers and dies by those forces of darkness, of the earthly 'I'. But death is followed by resurrection, the awakening into a world in which she no longer finds herself divided into seven qualities of her etheric being, but where she joins with the highest 'I', the cosmic 'I'.

* * *

So, following the mood of Christmas and the mood of fasting, there now follows the serious *Passion*-section of the fairy-tale, whose final climax comes in the mood of Good Friday (Snow-white's death) and

Easter Saturday (Snow-white lies in the glass coffin). All the degrees of the Christian story of suffering can be found again in this section of the fairy-tale. It is often said that these stages of suffering were the stages of initiation already in the pre-Christian Mysteries, and that they were later experienced as such in the Christian Mysteries. What Christ Jesus on the plane of outer earthly history had experienced in the Flagellation, the Crowning with Thorns and the Crucifixion, were already gone through in these early Mysteries, as in the later old Christian initiation, as specific etheric experiences. And this experience linked to these Imaginations of the Flagellation, the Crowning with Thorns, and the Crucifixion. In these pictures specific grades of becoming free were experienced by the pupil of the Mysteries, of releasing of one's etheric nature out of the physical part of the human entity. The pupil's ascent into higher worlds of the spirit took place by passing right through these degrees of Imaginative consciousness.

Thus Snow-white, too, becomes ever freer in her etheric being precisely through the suffering meeting with the binding, deeply oppressive power of the lower, earthly element; from stage to stage her higher being unfolds and develops. The pictures the fairy-tale presents clearly show the relationship to those early pre-Christian and Christian Imaginations. They only appear diminished in size through the child-sized context of the fairy-tale. And so the thongs of the whip in the fairy-tale Imagination have become the bodice laces, the points of the crown of thorns have become the teeth of the poisoned comb; nothing cleverly thought out is to be seen in these relationships, but with a destined necessity they place themselves out of their inherent reality before the inner eye when the soul meditatively looks on the connections of the fairy-tale.

It is significant that the wicked stepmother is only able to enter the spiritual world, the world 'beyond the mountains', in an ugly appearance. The inner being of the soul is here revealed outwardly, the good, loving element appears as beautiful, and the morally evil, hate, as ugly. The earthly beauty of the wicked queen appears here, consequently, in its true shape as ugliness, whereas Snow-white resting in the bed radiates before the dwarves in highest Sun-like beauty.

The effect of the bodice laces and of the comb can still be released by the dwarves; the power of the etheric world itself has the effect of becoming free. The etheric-spiritual is freed of its earthly entanglement. Only over that which is effected through the poisonous apple they have no power, over the death effected through the power of the [lower] 'I' —

one recalls the biblical story of the apple and the Fall of Man and its relationship to Golgotha. Only out of a still higher region, from the heights of the Sun, of the cosmic 'I' Itself, can the awakening come.

The episode of the entombment in particular is presented in the fairy-tale in a deeply moving fashion. The mourning of the dwarves who weep three days for Snow-white reminds us of other initiation stories, and with Snow-white we are dealing with an initiation. For Snow-white's death is no real death; the forces of death have no power over her pure Sun-being. The powers of decay do not touch her.

> They were going to bury her, but she still looked as fresh as a living being and her pretty cheeks were still rosy. 'We can't lower her into the dark ground,' they said and had a transparent glass coffin made so that one could view her from all sides, put her in it, and on it wrote her name in letters of gold and that she was a king's daughter.

And they placed the coffin on the top of a mountain, the mountain of initiation.

Early pre-Christian Mysteries are connected here in this initiation of Snow-white with the Christian Mystery of the future. Amongst the animals who also approach in order to weep for Snow-white — for deep in the cosmic context, the whole destiny of the animal world is connected with human destiny, with the Fall of Man, the death and resurrection of mankind — we find the owl and the raven, birds of death as messengers of the Mysteries, of the (ancient Greek and ancient Teutonic) past, the little dove comes as in the story of Noah as the messenger of the new life, of the Christian Mystery, where it appears again as the dove of the Grail.

And in particular Snow-white's glass coffin leads us deeply into the Mystery of the Grail. The Greek word *sarx* means 'flesh', the substance of the physical body. Looking at the physical body, it is itself the coffin in which our higher, spiritual, living being is buried. But Snow-white's initiation coffin is no ordinary coffin, but one made out of glass, a crystal-coffin. Pure crystal forces of the cosmos appear again in the physical world, which is penetrated and transformed by the Sun's being. The physical, mineral element, the original darkening of the etheric light, becomes again akin to the light, transparent for the light, like the mineral in the crystal, like the dark coal in the diamond. We recall how already the name Snow-white spoke to us of the mystery of the snow, in which cosmic-etheric, crystal beings of light weave and condense to the first, purest, virginal veil of earthly matter. Mysteries of the Christian resurrection live in this transformation of the physical element. The physical element transformed by the Sun-'I'-forces becomes again a vessel for the cosmic light, the Holy Grail.

In the picture of the crystal coffin we look at the physical body purified, transformed, radiated through with the power of the Sun. The physical is removed from the forces of decay. We see in the picture of the green 'bush' or 'shrub' the forces of budding life itself (the 'ether-body'). Highest Sun-'I'-force, 'the king's son', has received the coffin, the entombed body, from the etheric-earthly power, from the 'dwarves'. The 'servants' of the king's son—anthroposophy speaks of the relationship of the highest 'I' to the lower human members—knock against the shrub. The jolt effects the rejection of the poisonous foreign body; Snow-White who had lain in the sleep of death awakes. Easter, the resurrection, follows the lying in the grave on Easter Saturday. (In an Easter lecture in Dornach, Rudolf Steiner mentioned how in the early Mysteries a green branch presenting sprouting life was shown at a certain moment to the candidate lying in the coffin, during his awakening on the third day. We can clearly recognize this picture in the 'shrub' of the fairy-tale.)[74]

The highest treasure cannot be bargained for; it is given alone to the highest love, to the one worthy of it. And the awakened soul, the Eternal Feminine in us, Snow-white, finds the union with the Highest 'I', which from the regions of cosmic light, the highest cosmic love, stoops to her. In the picture of the 'chymical' wedding the mystery of the spiritual union is presented to us.

*   *   *

Why, it could be asked, after such heights of comic love are reached, does there still come this horrible sentence on the wicked queen at the end? But precisely here the fairy-tale seeks to be correctly understood. The confrontation with the evil powers governing the earthly situation forms something so essential that this ending could not be omitted. In that Snow-white selflessly takes on the controlling forces of evil in the earthly situation that bring death, these forces are overcome and changed; in the great fire of purification of the cosmic process they burn up of themselves. Evil is thereby of itself brought to its own end. What has divorced itself from the divine being of the world by entering into matter is taken up again by the original spiritual substance in this fire of purification. At this point we have to listen exactly to the language of the fairy-tale. If it really has to do with an outer sentence that some judge or other passes over the step-mother, then the above mentioned objection has a meaning. But no other power coerces her to appear before Snow-white; only she herself feels a compulsion that she cannot resist.

'At first she didn't want to go to the wedding at all, but that gave her no peace; she had to go and see the young queen.' And with this we can also understand at the end the words, 'Then she had to put on the red-hot slippers and dance until she dropped to the ground dead.' Here too nobody forces her; the shoes are only there for her; she can now not do otherwise than put them on. The feet, closest to the earth, are first burnt in the judging fire. Even in the pictures of the Earth's future in Klingsor's fairy-tale in Novalis' *Heinrich von Ofterdingen*, the forces of darkness opposing development dance themselves to death. That she has to endure the gaze of Snow-white, cannot pull herself away, in this lies the actual sentence on the wicked stepmother. Motionless from terror and fear she stands before the young queen. Only in this does the cosmic judgement consist, the decisive settlement with 'evil' in the cosmic process. The power of darkness in beholding the light, the Sun-being before Whom it is placed, cannot bear the radiating love from this Sun-being, that she injures herself in the rays of this love as in a fire.

And here, after we have followed the fairy-tale from Advent to Easter through its changing episodes and moods, we are led before a final mystery, linked to the time of year of St John's-tide that follows Easter. The spirituality of this St John's-tide, which in the early Mysteries was still celebrated as one of the greatest annual festivals, is the exact reversal of that which in the opening mood of the fairy-tale governs during Advent and Christmas. In this Advent and Christmas-tide a spirituality streams down to us full of grace, as we saw, and it lovingly covers the earthly plane. At St John's-tide, the reverse takes place; the earthly element streams towards the regions of cosmic warmth and of cosmic light. And in all this a judging cosmic power governs, which makes St John's-tide a time of crisis, of spiritual separation and decision. For out of the earthly everything arises that is full of guilt and error, that cannot be accepted by those pure ether-spheres, 'which alone can bear the guiltless on the glancing waves of Spirit' [Seasonal Epistle for St John's-tide of The Act of Consecration of Man]. In the St John's fire that which in the earthly sphere has become sterile and dead is burnt up; that which cannot live in the ether-spheres has to be burnt in the cosmic fire.

Supplement: 'Allerleirauh'

(From: Hermann Beckh, *John's Gospel: The Cosmic Rhythm — Stars and Stones*, tr. A. S. Leominster: Anastasi 2015, pp. 104–07, pp. 175, 383.)

The human *etheric* body, or 'life-body' — the 'Sun dress' in the Grimms' fairy-tale 'Allerleirauh', or 'All kinds of fur' — as 'colour-aura' is only perceptible to the clairvoyant eye, but in its spiritual essence it can also be comprehended in thinking. It stands closely connected with the activity of thinking itself. This human member is allocated to the cosmic realm. Unlike the physical body that connects the human being with the physical Earth, the etheric body connects with the 'aura of the Earth', with the living realm of the etheric in the plant, human and animal kingdoms, and with the living realm of the whole cosmos. The 'etheric body' [as the body of formative forces] is not to be understood out of merely spatial, earthly relationships, but out of cosmic relationships. It can be understood out of the essence and activity of the star-world with its lawfulness and cosmic rhythms. These influence the germination and growth of plants, and the essence of all time processes. As a cosmic 'being of time', not an earthly being of space, the etheric or life-body is to be conceived.

[In the little book *Der Ursprung im Lichte*, p. 17ff. (*Our Origin in the Light*, Temple Lodge, forthcoming), the author discusses how the essence of the etheric can be understood out of the mysteries of the biblical creation story, Goethe's archetypal plant, and the possibility to form an understanding out of the processes of plant growth and development.]

Amongst the Gospels, Mark's Gospel is allocated to the same cosmic realm and its rhythms. With John's Gospel this 'cosmic rhythm' is not so obvious. It is only found through looking at Mark's Gospel, at all the various relationships that in particular connect the Gospels of Mark and John.

Mark's Gospel relates to the etheric; Luke's Gospel relates to the human soul-astral realm. In the fairy-tale 'Allerleirauh', the 'astral body' appears as the 'Moon dress', which like the 'Sun dress' and the 'star dress' can be contained in a nutshell, that is, they are of a very fine, tender, super-earthly nature. This human 'astral body' is initially woven out of the essence of the starry, lunar, and planetary element. The human being shares the physical body, the 'dress made out of all kinds of furs' in the fairy-tale picture, with animal, plant and stone, the ether-body with animal and plant. The astral body, the bearer of conscious feeling, of the actual soul-element, is shared with the animals. Human beings are distinguished from the animals through the 'I' as the self-conscious human member. Naturally, because it is penetrated by the 'I', or ego, the soul-element of conscious feeling is different with human beings than with the animals. With the animals it is on the one hand duller, on the other hand, however, more cosmic—think of the wonderful feeling instinct of migratory birds. The 'astral element', the actual starry nature, appears stronger here. With the human being this starry, 'astral' element is obscured through the earthly consciousness of the lower ego.

[On the connection of each supersensory human member with the stages of cosmic development—'Ancient Saturn', 'Ancient Sun' and 'Ancient Moon', in the cosmological sense of *Esoteric/Occult Science*— compare the author's *Mark's Gospel: the Cosmic Rhythm*, p. 113. The 'Moon dress' of the fairy-tale, the astral body, is also allocated in this sense to the stage of evolution termed 'Ancient Moon', the 'Sun dress' to the 'Sun' and the stage of 'Sun-evolution'.]

The ether-body points us more towards the outer cosmic realm; the astral body points more to the inner soul, the 'inner starry world'. This inwardness has always been felt with Luke's Gospel as something essential.

As Matthew's Gospel belongs in a certain way to the human physical body, Mark to the etheric, Luke to the astral, John's Gospel belongs to the innermost principle, to the 'I' or ego. John's Gospel is pre-eminently the Gospel of the ego, the great message of the 'I'. We have to take the 'I' in the sublime, divine sense about which we actually only learn again out of John's Gospel. The next chapter will show how regarding the Mysteries of this 'I' as a new member of the human being, initially present only in seed-form in potential, John's Gospel speaks in all its chapters from ever new viewpoints. In the great I-AM sayings of Christ, in which all the future developments of humanity are included, this 'I'-Mystery has found its most concentrated expression. We saw this great 'I', this I-AM of Christ, aligned to the heavenly sign of the Scales, to the same sign governed by Venus Urania, by heavenly love. Venus in the Scales as the *love in the 'I'* is the governing motif of the whole of John's Gospel. One has only understood this 'I', this Johannine meaning of the 'I', when it is recognized how within it the *most inner place of the interior realm* lovingly joins together with the whole cosmic circumference.

In the language of the fairy-tale:

- the physical body is the 'dress of animal fur' (the 'coat of all kinds of fur'),
- the etheric body is the 'Sun dress',
- the astral body is the 'Moon dress',
- the 'I' is the '*starry body*', woven out of the rays of all the stars, and yet, like the Sun-dress and the Moon-dress, it can be hidden in a nutshell.
- The *physical* as the *earthly dress of the body*,
- the *etheric* as the *Sun-dress of life*,
- the *astral* as the *Moon-dress of light*,
- receives the 'I' as the *starry dress of love*, the fourth member of the human being, raising him/her to true humanity.

These pictures taken from the language of the fairy-tale really do agree with the inner being of John's Gospel. We only need to think of the Prologue (or 'cosmic Prelude') and, when we link the *Word in the primal beginning* with the 'Love in the primal beginning' (Dante's '*il primo Amore*'), the Incarnation of the Word (John 1:14) with physical corporeality, we find the whole fourfold human being (from which we proceeded in this section) as *body, life (v. 4), light (v. 6), and love*. And we may think of Novalis' words: '*Love really is in the "I"*, the ideal of every endeavour.'[75]

* * *

Here we find the context expressed in esoteric language, again in the plain, Johannine language of the Gospel, when we recall what was developed earlier (JG, Part One, Chapter 5) in this regard, referring to the language of fairy-tales.

- The primal situation on Ancient Saturn of the physical element in the human being appears then simply as the '*body*'.
- To it comes the Sun-filled etheric (the 'Sun dress' of the fairy-tale), the '*life*',
- in the lunar astral (in the 'Moon dress' of the fairy-tale) the '*light*'.
- And the earthly 'I' was completed in *love* (in the 'starry dress' of the fairy-tale), of which Novalis says: 'Love is the goal of world-history' (he means the whole evolution of the Earth), 'the Amen of the universe'.

* * *

Within this inner connection of the forces of the intercession of Christ coming to life in the stellar harmony, or music, we weave and work with them on the 'star-dress of love' of which we know that it is the 'I' in the language of fairy-tales that is expressed as the star-mystery of the 'I' (JG, Part One, Chapter 5). Here our feelings, awakening and coming to life with Christ's intercession flow together with them as expressed by Christian Morgenstern humanly so beautifully and simply in the poem 'Leis auf zarten Füßen naht es' [Soft on tender feet it approaches] in Wir fanden einen Pfad.

* * *

Some translations in English of the complete stories and tales collected by the Brothers Grimm:

- *The Complete Grimms' Fairy Tales*, Tr. Margaret Hunt (1831–1912), Intro. Padraic Colum, Folkloristic Commentary by Joseph Campbell. London: Routledge/ Pantheon Books Random House, 1992/97 *etc.*, Wordsworth Ed. Ltd 1998, and various reprint editions. Slightly archaic language.
- *The Grimm's German Folk Tales*, tr. Francis P. Magoun, Jr. and Alexander H. Krappe. Carbondale & Edwardsville: Southern Illinois Univ. Press/ London & Amsterdam: Feffer & Simons, Inc. 1960/ Arcturus Books 1969.
- *Brothers Grimm: The Complete Fairy Tales*. Tr., Intro & Annotated by Jack Zipes. London: Vintage Books 2007 (Jack Zipes also edits the *Oxford Companion to Fairy Tales*. OUP 2000).
- *Fairy Tales from the Brothers Grimm*. Tr. Phillip Pullman. Penguin Books 2013 (a substantial selection).

Review: Mysteries of the Material World

Rudolf Bind

Hermann Beckh, *Von Geheimnis der Stoffeswelt*. Dornach: Rudolf Geering Verlag. 1987. 140 pp.

This theme is dealt with on the highest level by the lawyer [Dr jur. Univ. of Heidelberg 1899, and subsequently judge], Professor of Oriental studies and Christian priest Hermann Beckh (1875–1937):

> *True alchymy begins in the human being and ends in the material world.* It carries within itself the mystery of metamorphosis, the transformation or transubstantiation of the earthly element. This change, working from the spiritual element takes place in the human being himself, at first invisibly and then progressively visibly, taking hold of earthly matter. That which in the writings of the alchymists and Rosicrucians can be found or guessed as verities leads ultimately into the Christian Mystery of the Resurrection.

This art and technique to transform what is incomplete to a higher level is based on the cultural realm of Egypt aligned to Hellenistic [thinking]. The use of language goes back to Paracelsus and Jakob Böhme, which partly lived on into the eighteenth century when one conversed in relationship to outer nature and man through the triad of *salt, mercury* and *sulphur*. It is noticeable that Rudolf Steiner liked to use this medieval, alchymical, pictorial language in the 1920s, particularly in those lectures where natural connections have to be presented as an organism, or as the connected realms of different entities. Rudolf Steiner once explained why it still makes sense today to express certain things using this ancient pictorial, conceptual language, in trying to feel and think their content in such a way as was still the custom right into the eighteenth century. It lies in the formation of the language that it is especially suitable for those who have died to take part in a mutual understanding between the living and those who have died. For 'especially amongst those who have gone through the portal of death, that which is vital in these concepts gradually becomes active and alive, it will become a language that is understandable to them and for which they are seeking' (GA 175. 20 March 1917).

The book under discussion by Hermann Beckh does not assume a reader who learns this language during the reading of the book, and who would like step by step to practice this view of the world. It is rather a rich concentrated bomb of content on the theme, surrounded by that well-known atmosphere made of content-extraction and cross-references that we knew in many diligent, seriously-learned treatises from our schooldays of yesteryear. This manner, held by the reins, swiftly striding out courageously and formatively in its reaching out, turns via the proven expert knowledge of the author to address those who condense into thought what is physically not yet graspable, fashioning this into meditative thinking, and who want to make this meditative, spiritual content their own. Last but not least, it is also for those who seek a spiritual-physical, universal natural scientific explanation, for the Mystery of metamorphosis (transubstantiation) and for sacramental life in general.

In this sense the book is a valuable, richly fashioned and orderly casket of treasure. This work by Beckh also helps one especially to follow up the relationship of Rudolf Steiner's presentations in individual lectures and even whole lecture-cycles on the Rosicrucian alchemical terminology and linguistic expressions right to the chymical processes; especially applicable are the lecture-courses on agriculture and astronomy, the lectures on the course of the year, but also those lectures where Steiner presents threefolding in the study of man and the social organism.

The present edition [1987] is an unaltered photo-mechanical reprint of the third edition of 1942. In the newly written Postscript the profound expert on matter, Willem F. Daems, succeeds in the space of three small pages to present an introduction and a detailed overview of the history of alchemy, as it is presented since the first post-Christian century in its Greco-Egyptian, Islamic and Latin streams.

Hermann Beckh, Orientalist, university lecturer, co-founder of The Christian Community, independent scholar

Born 4 May 1875 D-Nuremberg
Died 1 March 1937 D-Stuttgart

Gundhild Kačer-Bock
(Beckh's biographer, d. 2008)

(Tr. from the German:
http://biographien.kulturimpuls.org/detail.php?&id=48)

HERMANN BECKH, as a cultural researcher, exponent and lecturer, belongs to the exceptional figures of the Anthroposophical Movement before World War II.

He was the son of Eugen Beckh, co-owner of a factory for metal thread; his mother Marie, née Seiler [outlived her son]. His sister was 12 years his junior, to whom he was closely connected — she died in 1929. Beckh grew up in a prosperous, sheltered situation. He was a highly gifted yet sensitive child, who possessed a fine ability to differentiate colours, musical sounds and moods of nature. At five years old in the mountains, which he greatly loved all his life, he experienced a body-free condition that convinced him that human beings live through a pre-existent existence in the supersensory world.

At school it was apparent the he possessed an exceptional memory. The teaching methods put him off all subjects so that he could not decide on a profession. Nevertheless, a brilliant *Abitur* [school finals] earned him a scholarship to the Maximilianeum in Munich, where in particular the future members of the Civil Service studied. His original plan was to study national economics, because he hoped in this subject to be able to work for the social development of humanity. Through his fellow students he was increasingly stimulated to study law — he became by chance a judge, without a real decision to enter this profession, as he himself said. He ended his studies with his prizewinning work on *'Die Beweislast nach dem Bürgerlichen Gesetzbuch'* ['The burden of proof according to the code of civil law'], but practising as a judge he soon saw that it was impossible for him to be a judge all his life, when he actually wanted to help human needs. So at that moment when he stood directly before a position in the Civil Service, he broke from this professional path and began again from scratch. He began to study Indian and Tibetan philology, earned his doctorate in Berlin in 1907 with his work on Kalidasa's 'Meghaduta' ('The Cloud Messenger'). With his inaugural dissertation a year later with a further work on this text, he became one of the few specialists in the Tibetan language to teach at the University of Berlin and worked on the manuscripts in the *Königliche Bibliothek* (Royal Library).

In 14 December 1911 Beckh heard for the first time a public lecture by Rudolf Steiner (on the prophet Elijah; in GA 61, pp. 194–220). From then on he concerned himself intensively with Rudolf' Steiner's basic books. After a personal conversation with him, he became a member of the Anthroposophical Society at Christmas 1912. A few weeks afterwards Rudolf Steiner admitted him to the Esoteric School. During the course of 1913 he experienced a decisive climax in Steiner's career. In February the first Annual General Meeting of the newly-founded Anthroposophical Society, in August the Munich Summer Conference with Rudolf Steiner's Third and Fourth Mystery Dramas, the very first eurythmy performance, Rudolf Steiner's lecture as well as the Christmas lecture-cycle in Leipzig on *Christ and the Spiritual World* (GA 149), through which he received important impulses for the development of a renewed study of the stars. Despite the War, at Easter 1915 he could spend some days in Dornach and perceived the progress of the building of the Goetheanum.

In 1916 Beckh was called up for War-service. Shortly before the two small volumes of *Buddha und seine Lehre* in the Göschen series were published — the climax and in a certain sense also the end of his academic activities. First he was sent to the Balkans, after which he was called to the *Institut für Seeverkehr und Weltwirtschaft* [Institute for Shipping and World Economics] in Kiel, where he had to evaluate the economic articles in the Scandinavian Newspapers. For this he had to learn the Scandinavian languages, so that he had now mastered English, French, Italian, and the Scandinavian languages, along with Greek, Latin, Hebrew, Egyptian, Syriac, Sanskrit, Tibetan and Old Persian (the language of the *Avesta*). His War-service responsibilities — from August 1918 in the Berlin Foreign Service — lasted into the post-War period.

Alongside this he began again to lecture in the University of Berlin, but he saw that his professional future no longer lay in this realm, so he

searched for a possibility to work for the future of human development. He gave up his teaching post for Tibetan philology, and went on
leave from the University. When an extension of his leave was denied,
and instead of becoming an *'ausserordentlicher Professor'*, an 'extra-
ordinary Professor' (i.e. without a Chair), in November 1921 he wrote
to have his name withdrawn from the list of tutors. This was the end of
his academic career.

In 1920 Beckh offered himself as an anthroposophical lecturer. He
gave lectures on linguistics at the Anthroposophical Conference of 1921
and in March 1922 at the Berlin Conference, where he led the day on
philology [*Sprachwissenschaft*] under the theme 'From dead philology to
living philology'.

But the question of a satisfying life's task still remained open. When
Beckh then learned of the preparations for the founding of the Movement for Religious Renewal, he decided there and then to join the
founding group. Here the possibility was opened through the words
and language of a renewed rite to find a completely new access to the
word and to the sounds of speech. And he recognized that something
of a future Christianity was wanting to come into being, was what he
desired and intuited since as a 16-year-old he had attended a performance of Wagner's *Parsifal* in Bayreuth. Thus he was one of the oldest
of the 45 personalities who in September 1922 with Rudolf Steiner's
help called The Christian Community into life.

Still during the same year, Beckh moved to the newly built Urachhaus in Stuttgart. In the group of colleagues he took a special position
from the beginning. Unlike the others, he was not a priest serving a
congregation, but could engage his strengths in free activity as a tutor
in the Seminary, as lecturer, researcher and writer and still celebrate the
sacraments at various locations. This freedom to study enabled him
also to attend lectures at the Goetheanum in Dornach, to contribute in
cultural contexts such as the Schopenhauer Society and the Astrology
Association, for he was concerned to represent the aspects won out of
anthroposophy wherever people wanted to hear them.

The themes on which Beckh lectured ranged widely, initially proceeding from his academic work, considerations on language and
presentation of Eastern traditional wisdom. Soon he began to concern
himself with questions of music, particularly the music of Wagner and
the essence of tonality, and its connection with the forces of the stars,
making his realm of study these stellar forces in the sense of a renewing
of early Egyptian wisdom in astronomy and astrology. He sought to

discover the cosmic lawfulness of the zodiacal influences in their various effects and reflection in all areas, in the ancient languages and their sounds, in music and the colourful circle of musical keys, in the Mystery wisdom of earlier epochs of human history, in the Gospels and in human destiny. Thus his life's work did finally reveal a uniform thread.

Beckh was not a bookworm, but a human being with an impulsive temperament and a heart capable of enthusiasm. The little chores of daily life often presented obstacles, but his being and striving was always directed to the highest; thither he aimed to steer the thoughts of his listeners. He felt deeply connected with Rudolf Steiner and the Goetheanum. The experience of the Christmas Conference 1923 in Dornach of the General Anthroposophical Society, and his presence at Rudolf Steiner's 'Last Address' to the members on 28 September 1924 (in GA 238. Eng. tr. in *Mark's Gospel*, pp. 453–60, and *John's Gospel*, pp. 491–98) he felt as the climax of his life.

After he died on 1 March 1937, after a difficult period of suffering [cancer of the kidneys], Friedrich Rittelmeyer said of him, 'A singularly unique scholar, a rare wrestler for the spirit, an enthusiastic spirit-prophet has completed his rich life and has inscribed his name forever into the moving history of our time.'

Notes

1. T.H. Meyer, *The New Cain*. Forest Row: Temple Lodge 2017, p. 86.
2. See for example August Pauli's recollection quoted in G. Kačer-Bock, *Hermann Beckh. Life and Work*, tr. A. & M. Stott. Leominster: Anastasi 2016, p. 177.
3. Of the 48 founding priests ordained in September 1922, at least 31 had strong connections with Lutheran-Evangelical theology by having a Pastor as father, having studied Reformed theology in a university or having been ordained as a Lutheran-Evangelical Pastor before 1922. See R. F. Gädeke, *Die Gründer der Christengemeinschaft*. Dornach:Philosophisch-Anthroposophischer Verlag, 1992.
4. See for example, *Karmic Relationships*, Vol 2, Lecture 2. London: Rudolf Steiner Press 1974, pp. 28–9.
5. J. Scott, *The Woman in the Wilderness*. Pennsylvania: Middleton Books, 2005; see also R. Yoder, *Light Dawning. Gichtel, Boehme, Ephrata*. Holmes Publishing: Seqim, 2005.
6. For a general introduction see D. Hirst, *Hidden Riches*. London: Eyre & Spottiswoode, 1964, especially Chap. 3.
7. The published texts of Beckh's lectures have been collected and translated by A. Stott, *Hermann Beckh and the Spirit-Word*. Leominster: Anastasi 2015; *The Source of Speech*, Temple Lodge, 2019.
8. *The Collected Works of S.T. Coleridge* Vol. 12.1, Princeton University Press.
9. *Paradise Lost* Book 1, l.63.
10. See S.A. Konopacki, *The Descent into Words. Jakob Boehme's Transcendental Linguistics*. Ann Arbor: Karoma, 1979 for the best analysis.
11. S.O. Prokofieff, *Anthroposophy and The Philosophy of Freedom*, trans. M. St Goar, Temple Lodge 2009, pp. 22–3, 26.
12. Böhme uses the German verb *ringen* which plays on both 'circulating' as in a ring-dance and 'wrestling'.
13. Initial articles by Alan Stott on the chiasmic sentence structure of Rudolf Steiner's entire published prose appeared in the *Newsletter of the Performing Arts Section*, Dornach, Switzerland, RB 44, Easter 2006, pp. 27–30; RB 45, Michaelmas 2006, pp. 22-3 (also in German translation; available online https://srmk.goetheanum.org/ – further studies include an analysis of the 12-sentence rhythm that is equally present. Publication forthcoming.
14. The essential epitome of the waterstone as Christ in the human heart was produced by Johann Ambrosius Siebmacher, *Wasserstein der Weysen*, Frankfurt, 1619. This was translated into English as *Water Stone of the Wise*,

J.H., Oxon, for Giles Calvert, 1659 and bound with his translation of another seminal text, *Paracelsus his Aurora* – Ed.

15. Originally published in 1770; both Hermann Beckh and Emil Bock were able to take advantage of the edition issued by Pflüger-Verlag, München, in 1924. Currently available through Nabu Public Domain Reprints 2014.

16. Günther Wachsmuth, *The Etheric Formative Forces*, Vol. 1. London & New York, 1932 (download from: https://www.scribd.com/). See also Ernst Marti, *The Four Ethers*. Roselle: Schaumburg Publications. Inc., 1984. Marti claims Wachsmuth fails to differentiate the etheric forces from the formative forces. Download from several internet sites, e.g., at the time of writing: www.reddit.com/r/FringePhysics/.../ernst_marti_the_four_ethers_pdf/ https://keychests.com/item.php?v=bvdhrswofno

17. Jakob Böhme also observes in *De Incarnatione* that 'Paradise passed into mystery, and became for man a mystery or secret; although if he be born again of God, he dwells by the inner man in Paradise, but by the outer man in this world' (Chap. 3, para. 13. Tr. J.R. Earle) – Ed.

18. By 'wrath' (*Zorn*) Böhme did not mean an emotion. God reveals Himself in attributes among which there is something that today we might call dark 'energy', perhaps 'force' or 'forces'. The fall of Lucifer and the Fall of man, in Böhme's vision, intensified such unmanifested energy to the point that the *prima materia* became cold, dark, hard matter. *De incarnatione*, Chap. 4, para. 11 – Ed.

19. 'everywhere and nowhere': Novalis' insight is strongly supported by the well-known engraving included in Michael Maier's *Atlanta Fugiens* (1618), which depicts the cubical 'stone' lying everywhere in nature, surrounding the travellers who do not see it – Ed.

20. Rudolf Steiner reiterates this claim in *Theosophy of the Rosicrucians* (GA 99), Lecture 14, Munich, 6 June 1907, explicitly indicating that the controlled breathing process is 'the preparation of the Philosopher's Stone' which represents the fourth stage of the Rosicrucian training – Ed.

21. *Anthroposophie*, GA 234, Lect. 4, 1 Feb. 1924.

22. *Dīghanikāya*, Sāmaññaphalasutta. Rangoon: Burma Pitaka Association, 1984, p. 110.

23. Verlag für Schöne Wissenschaften: Dornach & Stuttgart, 1930, pp. 40–50.

24. Jakob Böhme repeatedly strove to describe the manifestation of the Divine Will within the feminine *Mysterium Magnum*, or first mother. The *Mysterium Magnum* is itself empty, nothing, but reflecting the Will as a mirror – Ed.

25. This work, originally published in Altona in 1785, has now reappeared with Hermann Barsdorf, Berlin, 1919. [Re-issued by Verlag Hermann Bauer, Freiburg im Breisgau, 1988. Also available, complete, in a smaller scale and only in black and white, in German and English translation, in: Paul M. Allen (Ed.) *A Christian Rosenkreutz Anthology*. Blauvelt, N.Y: Rudolf

Steiner Pub., 1968, pp. 211–328; hereafter page numbers in square brackets refer to this edition.]

26. Later chemists suggest the formula KNO^3.

27. Munich: Otto Wilhelm Barth Verlag, 1925; reissued Graz: Edition Geheimes Wissen, 2008.

28. See also Hermann Beckh, 'Mein Erlebnis mit Gustav Meyrink', *Die Christengemeinschaft* 1932, p. 369ff., Eng. tr. forthcoming in *Collected Articles of Hermann Beckh*, Temple Lodge.

29. See *Niels Bohr Collected Works*. Amsterdam: Elsevier 12 vols.; Berlin: Springer, 1924/2013.

30. *The Agriculture Course*, Koberwitz, 7–16 June 1924. GA 327.

31. For a short history of the Emerald Tablet and various translations, including that by Sir Isaac Newton, see <www.sacred-texts.com/alc/emerald>

32. *Goethe's Faust*, tr. W.H. van der Smissen. London & Toronto: Dent, and New York: Dutton, 1926. Scene 1, Night, 447–453.

33. *Colour*. Twelve lectures by Rudolf Steiner. Tr. John Salter & Pauline Wehrle. London: Rudolf Steiner Press, 2001, second edition, p. 188.

34. *Thus Spoke Zarathustra*, Part 2, 18 'On Great Events'.

35. See Rudolf Steiner, *True and False Paths of Spiritual Investigation*, Lecture 11, Torquay 22 Aug. 1924. GA 243. [All the pub. trs. of the passage in question are faulty. A more accurate translation is included in Lea van der Pals, *The Human Being as Music*. Leominster: Anastasi, 2014, pp. 120–23 — *Tr. addition.*]

36. Cf. the author's *The Language of Tonality*, Anastasi, 2015, p. 278.

37. The text is available in *Les Oeuvres de Nicolas Flamel*. Paris: Belfond, 1973.

38. *Das Geheimniss von dem Salz*, 1770, under the pseudonym Elias Artista Hermetica. Reprint available from Nabu Public Domain Reprints, 2014.

39. The identity of the Masonic author here is still debated, with many authorities accepting Beckh's recognition of J.A. Schmidt but others attributing the work to Hermann Fictuld (14 Jan 1700–c.1777). The 1737 text in question is not to be confused with the 'original' *Chrysopoeia*, a lengthy Latin poem on gold-making by Joannes Aurelius Augurellus (1441–1524) in 1515, subsequently translated into German by Valentin Weigel and reissued as *Vellus aureum et Chrysopoeia major et minor, das ist Güldene-Vliess*, Hamburg, 1716 — *Ed.*

40. The work is also attributed to Hermann Fichtuld who founded the Fraternity of the Golden and Rosy Cross in the 1750s — *Ed.*

41. Both translations pub. by Anastasi, 2015; Temple Lodge, forthcoming.

42. 'Working of the stars in earthly substances, experimental studies from the Biological Institute at the Goetheanum.' *Schriftenreihe der Natura*, Band I. Stuttgart: Orient-Occident Verlag, , 1927.

43. Novalis, *Notes for a Romantic Encyclopaedia*. Tr. David W. Wood, Albany: State University of New York Press, 2007, #339.

44. Stuttgart: Urachhaus, 1929/87, pp. 50-1.
45. The kabbalistic source *Aesch Metzareph* (Ch. 2), used by William Blake and taken up by the alchymists, comments on *ten different kinds of gold* that are found in the Tanakh. The gold of Genesis 2.12, *zahab tov*, is the ninth form — *Ed.*
46. This elliptic expression is a mantra, too. On the literal, purely grammatical side, it is simply personal pronouns — 'so' (the sandhi form of saḥ in conjunction with the next word) is third person singular, masculine; he. Then 'ham', which is 'aham' that loses the 'a' in conjunction with the final visarga (ḥ) of saḥ — first person singular; I. Thus, literally: he-I. He I [am].

    Note on 'he': Sanskrit uses genders like German: a river is feminine and the ocean is masculine. *Hamso* of course is also not the 'pausa' form, but the sandhi form. But the inversion seems a fairly old one — *Ed.*
47. Hermann Beckh is in agreement here with William Blake's *Jerusalem*. Blake's considerable knowledge of Indian traditions was demonstrated in the 1960s. He was certainly familiar with the early translations of Indian texts by Sir William Jones and Charles Wilkins, hence we also find explicit lotus images including the depiction of the sorrowful state of a mankind that is only half transformed into the swan, noticed here by Beckh. See for example Piloo Nanavutty, William Blake and the Hindu Creation Myths, in V. Pinto, ed., *The Divine Vision*. London: Gollancz, 1957 — *Ed.*
48. AV and RSV translates 'bdellium'; NIV 'aromatic resin'; Luther translates '*Bedellion*'.
49. Appearing thus in Luther's translation of the 'alchemical' verses of the O.T., Book of Daniel 2:41-3 — *Ed.*
50. Modern German *Ton* appears as *Thon* in Luther's tr. of Dan. 2:43-45. In the AV the translators opted for 'clay' — *Ed.*
51. See also the seventh seal, in *Occult Signs and Symbols*, Lecture 4. Stuttgart, 16 Jan. 1907. GA 101.
52. The term 'biosphere' was coined by geologist Eduard Suess as early as 1875 — *Ed.*
53. *Aus der Welt der Mysterien*. Basel: Verlag von Rudolf Geering,1927. Eng. tr. of the article in H. Beckh, MG, Appendix, pp. 465-72.
54. Rudolf Steiner. *Egyptian Myths and Mysteries*, Lecture 10, 12 Sept. 1908, Leipzig. GA 106: 'We should still point to something else. Human beings, when they arrived on Earth, were not yet endowed with the ego. Before the ego was mysteriously endowed into the astral body, other forces had possession of these bodies. Then the light-fluid astral body was permeated by the ego. Before the ego entered therein, the astral forces of divine-spiritual beings had been sent into man from without. The astral body was also present, but illuminated by divine-spiritual beings. The astral body was pure and bright, and it flowed around what was present as the rudiments of the physical and etheric bodies. It flowed around and

through these, and was quite pure. But egoism entered with the advent of the ego, and the astral body was darkened and lost its golden flow. This was progressively lost, until human beings had descended to the lowest point of the physical plane in the Greco-Latin age.

Then men had to consider how they could win back the pure flow of the astral body, and there arose in the Eleusinian mysteries what was known as the search for the original purity of the astral body. One aim of the Eleusinian mysteries, and also those of the Egyptians, was to recapture the astral body in its pristine golden flow. The quest for the Golden Fleece was one of the trials of the Egyptian initiations, and this has been preserved for us in the wonderful saga of the voyage of Jason and the Argonauts. We have seen the development. When the form of the lower organs still resembled the boats of which we have spoken, the astral body in the water-earth still had a golden sheen. In the water-earth the human astral body was permeated with golden light. The search for the astral body is portrayed in the voyage of the Argonauts. In a refined and subtle way we must bring the quest for the Golden Fleece into connection with the Egyptian myth.

55. Orient-Occident Verlag.

56. The original story is narrated in *The Visions of Zosimos*, first presented in Greek text and French tr. by M. Berthelot, 'Oeuvres de Zosime' in *Les alchimistes grecs*, 1888 — Ed.

57. Rosicrucian Christianity, Lecture 2, in *Esoteric Christianity and the Mission of Christian Rosenkreutz*, RSP, 2005, p. 65.

58. *Zanoni*. First ed. London: Saunders & Otley 1843; Createspace 2013. *A Strange Story*. London: Routledge, 1864; Shambala 1973.

59. Zürich: Grethlein 1927; München: Droemer Knaur, 1992; Bremen: Blessing 2003; EalaFrya- Literatur-Verlag, 2014; Dearbooks Verlag, 2014, etc. Eng. tr. *The Angel of the West Window*. Cambridge: Dedalus Ltd., 2010.

60. The name was chosen by the German chemist Martin Heinrich Klaproth in 1789. The fissionable qualities of Uranium were not discovered until 1934, three years after the publication of *Alchymie* — Ed.

61. A thorough study of Rudolf Steiner's presentations of Venus and Mercury is available online (2015):
http://wn.rsarchive.org/RelArtic/BobbetteRSW/steiner2_006.html

62. The original legend is connected to Eschenbach's *Parzifal* and found an artistic expression in E. Schuré's *Children of Lucifer*, performed for the International Congress of The Theosophical Society in Paris, 1906.

63. We find this indication in the above-mentioned text *Das Güldene Vlieẞ*, Nürnberg 1737, p. 7. There the list of famous alchymists and alchymical authors contains much that is remarkable. Besides the names known from the annals of alchemy, such as Morienus, Albertus Magnus, Arnold von Villanova (writer of *Flos Florum* and *Rosengarten der Weisen* — 'Rose Garden

of the Wise' and other alchymical works from the time of the Frederick II, the Emperor of Hohenstaufen, who himself was in favour of chymical studies), Geber, Avicenna (two famous Arabs), Rupescissa, Basilius Valentinus, Raymund Lullius, Theophrastus Paracelsus, and others, the following are also associated with alchymy: Hermes Trismegistos (the name of the primal initiator in Egypt), Pythagoras, Aristotle, Alexander (King of Macedonia), Plato, Socrates, Galenus, Hippocrates, Longinus, Euclid, Maria the prophetess, Thales of Miletos, Constantine, Alanus ab Insulis, Thomas Aquinas (concerning whom and his relationship to alchemy — Aquinas was a pupil of Albertus Magnus — see the above-mentioned novel of Gustav Meyrink, *The Angel of the West Window*). More detailed indications of alchymical authors can be found in the often-mentioned book by Schmieder.

64. The phrase 'light-flaming tincture' is found in *On the Incarnation*, Chap. 1, para 9. J.R. Earle unfortunately rendered this as 'light-flaming spirit'. Elsewhere Böhme uses other terms for the same insight, including 'the tincture of love' — *Ed. note.*

65. Leominster: Anastasi 2015, p. 41, p. 65f.

66. Those interested, and who perhaps miss the details in these contemplations, can find a very thorough account in 'A Golden Treatise about the Philosopher's Stone' (*Die Geheimen Figuren der Rosenkreutzer*, p. 38f. [p. 286f.]), which precedes the 'Parabola' like an introduction. It apparently takes a negative stance (all the substances discussed are initially dismissed). However, between the lines it contains much that is significantly positive. Wine, along with many other things, is mentioned. Concerning metals (quicksilver is taken as their 'beginning' and gold as their 'ending') antimony stands out especially (one recalls the famous book by Basilius Valentinus, *Der Triumphwagen des Antimoniums* [Leipzig, 1604]) and also aluminium, bismuth, magnesium, etc. Of non-metallic substances sulphuric acid in particular and several organic items play a role. The temporary rejection of all these substances occurs above all in relation to the saying of the alchymist Geber: 'He who has no knowledge by himself of the beginning of Nature is still far removed from this art.' [Quoted on p. 39 [p. 288] of *Die Geheimen Figuren*, in the text '*Ein güldener Traktat vom Philosophischen Steine.*']

67. Entry 79 in *Notes for a Romantic Encyclopaedia*, 1798–9.

68. *From Jesus to Christ*, Lect. 8. The 'other connection' is the formation of the 'Phantom' body — *Ed.*

69. See Friedrich Benesch, *Der Turmalin.* Stuttgart: Urachhaus, 2000/03.

70. See *Hastings Dict. of the Bible*, rev. ed. Grant & Rowley. Edinburgh: T&T Clark, 1963.

71. Novalis. *Schriften von Ludwig Tieck und Friedrich von Schlegel*, 1826, (II. Aesthetik und Literatur), p. 129.

72. 'The Way of Life.' From the German of Goethe (tr. Arthur John Lockhart in *The Bird of the Cross and other Poems*. Winterport, Maine: C.R. Lougee, 1909, pp. 21–22.) The following note is appended: 'Johann Wolfgang von Goethe, the illustrious poet of Germany, was initiated into Masonry on St John's Eve, in 1780. In 1830 the Masons of Weimar celebrated his Semi-centennial; and the venerable Companion was pleased to honour them with a mark of his esteem in the form of a poetical composition.' Other authorities claim this undated poem was written around 1815, with the Hamburg edition placing it on 5 December 1815 for the reception of August v. Goethe into the Weimar Lodge. Beckh quotes verses 2–6. Here is the complete text:

> *Symbolum*
>
> *Des Maurers Wandeln,*
> *Es gleicht dem Leben,*
> *Und sein Bestreben,*
> *Es gleicht dem Handeln*
> *Der Menschen auf Erden.*
>
> *Die Zukunft decket*
> *Schmerzen und Glücke.*
> *Schrittweis dem Blicke;*
> *Doch ungeschrecket*
> *Dringen wir vorwärts.*
>
> *Und schwer und ferne*
> *Hängt eine Hülle,*
> *Mit Ehrfurcht, stille*
> *Ruhn oben die Sterne*
> *Und unten die Gräber.*
>
> *Betracht' sie genauer*
> *Und siehe, so melden*
> *Im Busen der Helden*
> *Sich wandelnde Schauer*
> *Und ernste Gefühle.*
>
> *Doch rufen von drüben*
> *Die Stimmen der Geister,*
> *Die Stimmen der Meister:*
> *Versäumt nicht zu üben*
> *Die Kräfte des Guten!*
>
> *Hier winden sich Kronen*
> *In ewiger Stille,*
> *Die sollen mit Fülle*
> *Die Tätigen lohnen!*
> *Wir heißen euch hoffen.*

73. From Klingsohr's Tale in *Heinrich von Ofterdingen*.
74. Both Rudolf Steiner and Hermann Beckh were aware that the 'green branch' also refers to the verdant acacia that marked the burial place of Hiram Abiff in the initiation of a Master Mason.
75. *Romantic Encyclopedia*, #835.

The Works of Prof. Hermann Beckh
Dr jur. et phil.

'An abundance of books came into existence whose significance perhaps will only be properly appreciated in the future.'

(Lic. Emil Bock, 'Hermann Beckh' in *Zeitgenossen Weggenossen Wegbereiter*, Stuttgart: Urachhaus 1959. 132)

*

Die Beweislast nach dem Bürgerlichen Gesetzbuch
'The burden of proof according to the Code of Civil Law'
Prize essay, awarded distinction from the Law Faculty the University of Munich
München und Berlin 1899. Download: http://dlib-pr.mpier.mpg.de/m/kleioc/0010/exec/books/%22103926%22/

Ein Beitrag zur Textkritik an Kālidāsas Meghadūta
'A contribution to the text criticism of Kālidāsa's Meghadūta'
Doctorate dissertation approved by the Department of Philosophy of the University of Berlin 1907.

Die tibetische Übersetzung von Kālidāsas Meghadūta
'The Tibetan translation of Kālidāsa's Meghadūta'
Edited and with a German translation, Berlin 1907/2011.

Beiträge zur tibetischen Grammatik, Lexikogaphie, Stilistik und Metrik
Habilitationsschrift. Berlin 1908.
'Contributions to Tibetan grammar, lexicography, style and metre'
Inaugural dissertation.

Udānavarga
A collection of Buddhist sayings in the Tibetan language.
Berlin 1911 (also reprinted by Walter de Gruyter, 2013).

Verzeichnis der tibetischen Handschriften
'Catalogue of Tibetan MSS in the Royal Library in Berlin' (Vol. 24 of the Manuscript Catalogue). First division: Kanjur (Bhak-Khgur).
Berlin 1914/2011/14.

Buddha und seine Lehre
'Buddha and his Teaching.' Vol. 1: The Life. Vol. 2: The Teaching.
Sammlung Göschen. Berlin & Leipzig 1916. Third edition 1928.
Later one-volume editions, Stuttgart: Urachhaus 1958/98/2012. Tr. into Dutch and Japanese.
Eng. tr. *Buddha's Life and Teaching*, Temple Lodge 2019.

'*Rudolf Steiner und das Morgenland*'
in *Vom Lebenswerk Rudolf Steiners*
Ed. Friedrich Rittelmeyer, München: Chr. Kaiser 1921
Reprint by HP, Univ. of Michigan (www.lib.umich.edu) (download: www.archive.org).
Eng. tr. in *Hermann Beckh and the Spirit-Word*, Leominster: Anastasi 2015. Pp. 33–65.

- *Der physische und der geistige Ursprung der Sprache*

The physical and the spiritual origin of language. Stuttgart 1921.

- '*Es werde Licht!*' 'Let there be light!'

The primal biblical words of creation and the primal significance of the sounds in the light of spiritual science. Stuttgart 1921.

- *Etymologie und Lautbedeutung*

Etymology and the significance of speech sounds in the light of spiritual science.
Stuttgart 1922/2013.
All three essays on language (above) reprinted in
Neue Wege zur Ursprache, Stuttgart 1954.
Eng. tr. *The Source of Speech*, with two extra essays 'Indology and Spiritual Science'. Temple Lodge, 2019.

Anthroposophie und Universitätswissenschaft
'Anthroposophy and University Knowledge'
Breslau 1922. Eng. tr. in *Hermann Beckh and the Spirit-Word*, Leominster: Anastasi 2015. Pp. 71–101.

Vom geistigen Wesen der Tonarten
The Essence of Tonality: An Attempt to view musical Problems in the Light of Spiritual Science. With diagrams. Breslau 1922. Third edition 1932. Eng. tr. Leominster: Anastasi 2008.

Der Ursprung im Lichte. Bilder der Genesis
Our Origin in the Light: Pictures from Genesis. Stuttgart 1924. Eng. tr. Temple Lodge, forthcoming.

Von Buddha zu Christus
From Buddha to Christ
Stuttgart 1925 (tr. in Norwegian, Oslo 1926); Eng. tr. selections Floris Books 1978.
New Eng. tr. of full text, Temple Lodge 2019.

Das neue Jerusalem
'The New Jerusalem'
A poetic work, in the collaborative work *Gegenwartsrätsel im Offenbarungslicht* ('Problems of the present in the light of revelation'), Stuttgart 1925. Eng. tr.

incl. in *John's Gospel: The Cosmic Rhythm – Stars and Stones*. Leominster: Anastasi 2015. Pp. 459–77; Temple Lodge, forthcoming; also in *Alchymy*, Temple Lodge, 2019.

Der Hingang des Vollendeten
'The Passing of the Accomplished One and His Nirvāṇa (Mahāparinibbāna Sutta of the Pali canon').
Translated and with an introduction. Stuttgart 1925/60. Eng. tr. *Buddha's Passing* Temple Lodge, forthcoming.

Zarathustra
Stuttgart 1927
Eng. tr. with additional articles, include in *From the World of the Mysteries*, Temple Lodge, forthcoming.

Aus der Welt der Mysterien
From the World of the Mysteries
Seven articles (reprinted). Basel 1927. Eng. tr. with *Zarathustra*, Temple Lodge, forthcoming.

Der kosmische Rhythmus im Markus-Evangelium
Mark's Gospel: The Cosmic Rhythm
Basel 1928/60/97. Eng. tr. Leominster: Anastasi 2015; Temple Lodge, forthcoming.

Der kosmische Rhythmus, das Sternengeheimnis und Erdengeheimnis im Johannes-Evangelium
John's Gospel: The Cosmic Rhythm – Stars and Stones
Basel 1930. Eng. tr. Leominster: Anastasi 2015; Temple Lodge, forthcoming.

Das Christus-Erlebnis im Dramatisch-Musikalischen von Richard Wagners 'Parsifal'
The Parsifal=Christ=Experience in Wagner's Music Drama
Stuttgart 1930. Eng. tr. with 'Richard Wagner and Christianity' (1933) and essays by Emil Bock (1928) and Rudolf Frieling (1956), Leominster: Anastasi 2015.

Vom Geheimnis der Stoffeswelt (Alchymie)
Alchymy: The Mystery of the Material World
Basel 1931/37/42/2007/13. Eng. tr. with appendices, Temple Lodge 2019.

Der Hymnus an die Erde
The Hymn to the Earth: From the Old Indian Atharvaveda: A memorial to the oldest poem and to the early Aryans.
Germ tr. and commentary. Stuttgart 1934/60. Eng. tr. Temple Lodge, forthcoming.

Psalm 23 aus der Heiligen Schrift
Psalm 23: Newly translated from the original text and set to music, op. 7.
Stuttgart 1935.

Die Rosen von Damaskus
The Roses of Damascus. 'Thibaut von Champagne'. The ballad by Conrad Ferdinand Meyer. For solo high voice with piano accompaniment set to music, op. 8. Stuttgart 1937.

Die Sprache der Tonart
The Language of Tonality in the Music from Bach to Bruckner with special reference to Wagner's Music Dramas
Stuttgart 1937/87/99. Eng. tr. Leominster: Anastasi 2015; Temple Lodge, forthcoming.

Richard Wagner und das Christentum
Richard Wagner and Christianity
Stuttgart 1933. Eng. tr. incl. in *The Parsifal=Christ=Experience in Wagner's Music Drama*. Leominster: Anastasi 2015; Temple Lodge, forthcoming.

Indische Weisheit und Christentum
Indian Wisdom and Christianity
Articles: 10 reprinted and 9 from the literary estate.
Stuttgart 1938. Eng. tr. Temple Lodge, forthcoming.

Der Mensch und die Musik
The Human Being and Music
A recently discovered history of music in Ms:
Five chapters pub. in three articles in *Die Europäer*, Basel 09.2005/09.2006/ 02.2007-08.
http://www.perseus.ch/archive/category/europaer/europaer-archiv
Full restored text translated into English, Temple Lodge 2019.

Collected Articles and Essays translated into English, two volumes, forthcoming.

Biography:
Hermann Beckh: Life and Work
by Gundhild Kačer-Bock (d. 2008)
Stuttgart 1997. Eng. tr. Leominster: Anastasi 2016.

Hermann Beckh and the Spirit-Word:
Orientalist, Christian Priest and Independent Scholar
- A. Stott, 'Hermann Beckh and the Twenty-First Century'
- H. B., 'Rudolf Steiner and the East'
- H. B., 'Anthroposophy and University Knowledge'
- H. B., 'Meeting Rudolf Steiner'
- Numerous appreciations by Beckh's colleagues and his biographer; introducing the *Collected Works of Hermann Beckh*

A note from the publisher

For more than a quarter of a century, **Temple Lodge Publishing** has made available new thought, ideas and research in the field of spiritual science.

Anthroposophy, as founded by Rudolf Steiner (1861-1925), is commonly known today through its practical applications, principally in education (Steiner-Waldorf schools) and agriculture (biodynamic food and wine). But behind this outer activity stands the core discipline of spiritual science, which continues to be developed and updated. True science can never be static and anthroposophy is living knowledge.

Our list features some of the best contemporary spiritual-scientific work available today, as well as introductory titles. So, visit us online at **www.templelodge.com** and join our emailing list for news on new titles.

If you feel like supporting our work, you can do so by buying our books or making a direct donation (we are a non-profit/charitable organisation).

office@templelodge.com

☀ TEMPLE LODGE
For the finest books of Science and Spirit